KU-313-340

Advance Praise for **MARX, CAPITAL, and EDUCATION**

"This book boldly interrogates the internal contradictions of capital with the aim of galvanizing a critical pedagogy of becoming, a pedagogy capable of providing the conceptual and analytic resources necessary to locate and pry open spaces in education from which to push those contradictions to their breaking point so as to transform capitalism into communism. The authors patiently explain the dialectical logic of capital's internal contradictions that incline capital towards self-negation, paying particular attention to capital's compulsive quest for surplus value; they deepen this explanation with an exploration of Marx's appropriation of dialectics from Hegel. Setting these explanations in motion and keeping capital's thirst for surplus value firmly in view, Malott and Ford confront and intervene in some of the main debates related to education under capital, including the relation between educational labor and the reproduction of capitalist social relations, and the relation between race and class. This book propels forward the revolutionary struggle for liberation from class society."

—Deborah P. Kelsh, *Professor of Teacher Education, The College of Saint Rose*

"Malott and Ford point to the horizon of possibilities that open up when Marx is put back into Marxism. Their bold advocacy of critical pedagogy as a self-conscious movement towards communism is a welcome antidote to the bourgeois fluff that has come to pass as 'critical' in education for too long. *Marx, Capital, and Education* is written by revolutionary educators for revolutionary educators."

—Grant Banfield, *Lecturer, Faculty of Education, Humanities and Law,*
Flinders University, South Australia

"Malott and Ford present a rigorous theoretical framework grounded in the actual practice of communist movement(s). Their approach to educational pedagogy is a must-read for anyone with a radical consciousness seriously concerned with not just interpreting, but changing the world."

—Eugene Puryear, *author of* Shackled and Chained: Mass Incarceration
in Capitalist America; *Organizer with the ANSWER Coalition*

"Malott and Ford in this exceptional work place capitalism 'squarely within the crosshairs.' Vague talk concerning issues of social justice is replaced with concrete explorations of our present historical moment within the horizon of communism and educators' place in moving toward that horizon within a process of a critical pedagogy of becoming. This book will move critical thinkers toward the horizon. It is about time."

—William M. Reynolds, *Associate Professor of Curriculum, Foundations, and Reading, Georgia*
Southern University

"Twenty-five years after the collapse of the Soviet Union, world 'leaders' continue to directly and indirectly promote anticommunist disinformation and propaganda. Today one is casually and smugly dismissed as passé or out of touch if they are still 'gullible' enough to fight for communism. Opposing this relentless capital-centered offensive which depoliticizes people and intensifies anticonsciousness, Malott and Ford have boldly put communism on the agenda. With courage, conviction, and serious analysis they show how and why existing political-economic arrangements can and must be replaced by a human-centered society and economic system, a world free of exploitation, alienated relations, and the division between mental and manual labor. To this end, the authors skillfully sketch the organic connections between critical pedagogy, transformation, and Marxist and Hegelian dialectics in order to advance 'a pedagogy of becoming.' Here the future lies within the present and negation is affirmation. But Malott and Ford remind us at every turn that this does not mean that phenomena unfold deterministically."

–*Shawgi Tell, Associate Professor of Education, Department of Social and Psychological Foundations of Education, Nazareth College*

"This book is a weapon to be used not merely against capital, but in the revolutionary struggle to overthrow capitalism and realize a communist future that enables the becoming of humanity. In an era in which Marxist educational theorizing is making a comeback, Malott and Ford represent the best of a new generation of revolutionary thinkers who do not settle for merely interesting academic inquiry, but rather illustrate how deep intellectual inquiry can inform answers to questions about how we can teach, learn, and take action in the construction of a proletarian offensive in the global class war. Malott and Ford unapologetically embrace the goal of creating a new set of social relations that enable the absolute movement of becoming, that is communism. They put capitalism in the crosshairs and refuse to take cover under the empty shells that democracy, social justice, or domesticated critical pedagogy have become. Instead they return to Marx, offering crystal clear theoretical and practical responses to questions at the heart of conversations about how we can create not only new pedagogies, but a new world, free from the scourge of capitalism."

–*E. Wayne Ross, Professor, Faculty of Education, University of British Columbia*

"This is a hugely important and impressive book by...two increasingly influential revolutionary Marxist theorists/activists. They assert and closely argue that 'in order for education to contribute to the generation of a counterpower it has to place capital squarely in its crosshairs.' They open up the field of possibilities for revolutionary education, enabling the imagination of 'a world without the exploitation and oppression that characterizes capital.' This book is hard-hitting and uncompromising. It is scholarly. It is activist. It is a remarkable addition to contemporary critical education and Marxist theory."

–*Dave Hill, Professor of Education Research, Anglia Ruskin University, England;*
Chief Editor of the Journal for Critical Education Policy Studies;
Co-founder and Co-organizer of the annual International Conference on Critical Education

WITHDRAWN FROM
THE LIBRARY

UNIVERSITY OF
WINCHESTER

THE UNIVERSITY OF
WINCHESTER

Martial Rose Library
Tel: 01962 827306

To be returned on or before the day marked above, subject to recall.

KA 0426512 2

MARX,
CAPITAL,
and EDUCATION

UNIVERSITY OF WINCHESTER
LIBRARY

Narrative, Dialogue,
and the Political
Production of Meaning

Michael Peters & Peter McLaren
Series Editors
Vol. 5

The Education and Struggle series is part of the Peter Lang Education list.
Every volume is peer reviewed and meets
the highest quality standards for content and production

PETER LANG
New York • Bern • Frankfurt • Berlin
Brussels • Vienna • Oxford • Warsaw

Curry Stephenson Malott and Derek R. Ford

MARX, CAPITAL, and EDUCATION

Towards a Critical Pedagogy of Becoming

PETER LANG
New York • Bern • Frankfurt • Berlin
Brussels • Vienna • Oxford • Warsaw

Library of Congress Cataloging-in-Publication Data
Malott, Curry Stephenson.
Marx, capital, and education: towards a critical pedagogy of becoming /
Curry Stephenson Malott, Derek R. Ford.
pages cm. — (Education and Struggle: Narrative, Dialogue
and the Political Production of Meaning; v. 5)
Includes bibliographical references and index.
1. Critical pedagogy. 2. Capitalism and education.
3. Marx, Karl, 1818–1883. I. Ford, Derek R. II. Title.
LC196.M22   370.11′5—dc23   2015009636
ISBN 978-1-4331-3112-7 (Hardcover)
ISBN 978-1-4331-3111-0 (Paperback)
ISBN 978-1-4539-1602-5 (e-book)
ISSN 2168-6432

Bibliographic information published by **Die Deutsche Nationalbibliothek**.
Die Deutsche Nationalbibliothek lists this publication in the "Deutsche
Nationalbibliografie"; detailed bibliographic data are available
on the Internet at http://dnb.d-nb.de/.

UNIVERSITY OF WINCHESTER

Cover art: "Cracked Grid" by Sarah Pfohl

The paper in this book meets the guidelines for permanence and durability
of the Committee on Production Guidelines for Book Longevity
of the Council of Library Resources.

© 2015 Peter Lang Publishing, Inc., New York
29 Broadway, 18th floor, New York, NY 10006
www.peterlang.com

All rights reserved.
Reprint or reproduction, even partially, in all forms such as microfilm,
xerography, microfiche, microcard, and offset strictly prohibited.

Printed in the United States of America

This book is dedicated to all of the proletarian teachers, students, and fighters in the global class war.

CONTENTS

FOREWORD

BEING AND BECOMING COMMUNIST: TOWARD A REVOLUTIONARY CRITICAL PEDAGOGY OF BECOMING

Is communism the indisputable and irrevocable horizon of the present historical juncture? This question is of grave discernment for humanity. *Marx, Capital, and Education* represents an extended and exhilarating exegetical "yes" to this question.

The political trajectory of this book alone should explode the mainstream debate over education into a frenzy of contradictions, omissions, and analytic paralyses, sending shards of hope flying through the air like Fourth of July bottle rockets whistling *The Internationale*. But honesty demands that we ask: What fate will such a book truly enjoy in a field in which critical pedagogy continues to be burdened by the scars of its compliance with the neoliberal academy and where tinkering with capitalism underwrites the *ne plus ultra* defiant act of the critical pedagogue? This is an especially important question in a world in which capitalism remains synonymous with democracy, and the struggles for democracy effectively mean democracy for the capitalist class alone. In the short run, *Marx, Capital, and Education* will obviously both polarize and mobilize. It will polarize the left, provoking the majority of liberal and left liberals to run shrieking from its essential premises and to take refuge on the wrong side of the ramparts (which is almost always the side populated with the best of intentions and the most highbrow of qualifications). As soon as readers learn that the authors are unrepentant "communists," they will earmark the book for the office dustbin or for the bonfire at the next church retreat, after the Bible trivia games and the speed-dating event for the parish singles. Or else they will blame the book when they rush out of the prayer tent screaming after being bitten by the yellow timber rattlesnake they were handling during the service.

Ignoring *Marx, Capital, and Education* because of its communist foundations comes at a price, the least of which is forfeiting an important opportunity to learn what it takes to be a transformative educational warrior in a global war. In rejecting *a priori* the book's critiques and strategies for the revolutionary transformation of our planet, a reluctant public will impotently stand by in frozen disdain and under pain of remaining oblivious to what is most specifically human about us, only prolonging the agony of the wretched of the earth. Here, as is too often the case, a formidable indifference to the suffering of others will form the blackest residue of our being.

I have been an educator since 1974, and during the ensuing years up to the present, I have rarely encountered an educational book like *Marx, Capital, and Education* that speaks so clearly and potently the truth about what it will take to bring justice to the immiserated of this world. *Marx, Capital, and Education* will be a terribly uncomfortable book for most educators to read because the mass media and the rest of the ideological state apparatuses will have already predisposed them to reject it outright, probably within the first few pages.

Education is a decidedly conservative field, after all, and even those few truly radical philosophical and theoretical books that have made it onto the library shelves of colleges of education—Freire's *Pedagogy of the Oppressed* immediately comes to mind—have been politically domesticated in the process of bringing such works to bear on the actual service of teaching. Freire's ideas have been uprooted from their soil in working-class communities and repotted in reading lists in graduate schools more for decoration than for substance, like the glass terrarium orchid vases that brighten up the exposed brick walls of urban lofts. Transformed into luxurious discursive amenities for conversations taking place in graduate seminars and student lounges, these ideas eventually become refunctioned in the service of student embourgeoisement. Academic careers in the United States depend upon a reflex demonization of Marx for many reasons, not least of which has to due with the fact that, when scrutinized under a Marxist optic, the work of many scholars is revealed to be as porous as the cell membranes of the Wicked Witch of the West, who melted into oblivion on contact with water in *The Wizard of Oz*. Hence, most attacks on Marx come from a dismissal of his work as an example of economic reductionism or teleological theorizing, from the claim that his writings prefigure the historical inevitability of the dictatorship of the proletariat or that all alienation will cease as soon as factories collectivize. While some critical educators give ground for the reproach of being against Marxism, this attitude is due more to an incomplete understanding of Marx than of boasting a greater sociological understanding than the old bearded devil himself. These critics frequently make their claims while ignoring Marx's own writings and avoiding works that have already been written by Marxists that have already addressed these issues and put them to rest.

To write a book such as *Marx, Capital, and Education* requires courage and steadfastness to the cause of liberation, especially during these unholy times of national security corporate capitalism that has begotten the national security state. Likely, the book will be featured prominently on the review lists of left academic journals eager to bring a Marxist optic to the field of education, of which this book clearly ranks among the most pathfinding and important, and this will be a good thing. But this is a book that demands to be read and rigorously digested not only by professional intellectuals but by teachers who work in institutions ranging from kindergartens to universities and by radical organizers. Hence, the importance of getting this book into the hands of as many educators and activists as possible as quickly as possible.

In my own educational life, it took me many years to grasp and to be comfortable with the positions taken in *Marx, Capital, and Education*. As a former comparative symbologist with a penchant for what I called a "critical postmodernism," there were many theoretical and political hurdles that were necessary for me to overcome in order to be able to put forward positions in my post–1995 work similar to or compatible with those of Malott and Ford. First and foremost, I needed to engage in the original works of Marx and Marxist scholars while developing a thorough understanding of the arguments made by Marx's defenders and critics; second, I needed to be able to understand Marx's contribution to a critique of political economy when read against the prevailing trends in philosophy, social theory, political science, and economics, including their postmodern and neoliberal variants; and third, I needed to be able to weigh Marxist critiques of education against critiques employing other theoretical and philosophical trajectories. The point that I am trying to make is that engaging *Marx, Capital, and Education* by the rank-and-file educator will require a steadfast commitment to undertaking a long and difficult journey of discovery. This is a journey that I believe is absolutely necessary if humanity is not to sink into a barbarism the likes of which we are loath today to contemplate, simply because the image we are likely to conjure will be worse than all the ravages of historical wars of empire combined. Reading this book will serve as an important and necessary conceptual catapult in helping us to contemplate our being-in-the world as activist protagonistic agents, to grasp the nature of what it means to be human, and to reveal precisely what our normalized and normalizing approaches to everyday life are meant to conceal.

I opened this preface by saying that I believe this book will both polarize and mobilize. How, then, will it mobilize readers? In its brilliant adumbration of neoliberalism as a counterrevolutionary strategy within capitalism and its perceptive attribution of liberation to the realization of a communist society, it will immediately have the effect of assisting radical left educators who have already committed themselves to a Marxist analysis in their various efforts to mobilize communities against corporate efforts to privatize education and transform education into a subsector of the economy. But I believe it will have an even larger and more enthusiastic audience outside the United States and that once its international influence is felt, it will then be reengaged enthusiastically by larger and growing numbers of educators in the United States as a means of rerooting Marxism here among U.S. educators. Hence, I believe there should be efforts made to have this book translated into as many languages as possible as soon as possible.

Students in colleges of education are not that much different from students in other fields: they seek secure employment, they want to raise families and contribute to society, and they want to enjoy the fruits of their hard work. Admittedly, most of them don't want to be overwhelmed by world events or engaging in the arduous work necessary to acquire the skill sets that will enable them to read the word and the world with a critical eye toward the suffering masses of humanity, the ranks of which are expanding exponentially with each passing decade. Everyday life—raising a family, holding down a job, keeping oneself and one's loved ones healthy—is a daunting enough challenge without having to carry an additional burden of research and analysis, let alone engage in international proletarian struggle. Yet the consequences of not engaging in such a struggle are growing direr with each and every passing day. We *cannot* afford *not* to engage in such a struggle since the future of humanity depends upon us, upon all of us. There is no more room for dispute between capitalists and wage earners. There is only room for action. Hence the book *Marx, Capital, and Education*.

In the remaining space of the preface, I want to summarize what I believe to be some distinguishing characteristics of this book and why it ranks, in my mind, among the best books on Marx and education to date, if not the best. And why I believe that this book can serve to reroute Marxist theory into critical pedagogy and education more generally.

Marx, Capital, and Education removes itself from generic conventions in the Marxist educational literature that precedes it. Whereas many books on education attempting to conscript Marx into the service of educational reform point to a socialist or democratic alternative to capitalism, Malott and Ford mince no words about the importance of a communist destination for humanity. They make no bones about the fact that this is a book written by two radical educators, two communist intellectual activists who share little affinity with the haute-bourgeois intellectuals who have made careers out of criticizing critical pedagogy. They have written this book for the sole purpose of furthering the international proletarian struggle. Because the Soviet Union and the Eastern Bloc states are now caricatured as totalitarian dictatorships, and because Marx is judged, in turn, to be *ipso facto* a dangerous demagogue as a result of these perceptions, Malott and Ford certainly have their work cut out for them.

Malott and Ford describe communism, after Marx, as the "absolute moment of becoming." As historical materialists, they see education in this context as cultivating the process of becoming more fully human and assert that communism is the only viable alternative for achieving such a goal. What is so crucially important about this book is that Malott and Ford articulate a humanism that opens up rather than closes down the corpus of writings by Marx. First, unlike many post-Marxists, they do not reject the ontological category of the subject itself. They perceive revolutionary subjectivity to be immanent in the very structure of capital that it aims to revolutionize. Second, while they realize that there may never be a fully resolutive form of the social, they remain undaunted in their strategic priority of engaging in a protracted class struggle. Third, by taking an objectivist position, they do not reject the idea that society can be considered an immanent totality and that there are immanent tendencies to capitalist development that necessitate a particular form of revolutionary subjectivity that privileges the working class. And last, they do not retreat from the idea that history has a subject and that the proletariat has a special relationship to progressive politics.

These facts alone will make it difficult for liberals and left liberals to join in support for the kind of orthopraxis called for in this book. Left liberals stop short in advocating for the destruction of capitalism and instead call for the restoration of the primacy of labor over capital, workers' self-management, direct democracy, social welfare initiatives, management/labor alliances, housing cooperatives for the poor as an antidote to gentrification, effective investment programs, disinvestment, corporate responsibility, an end to the oligopolistic price fixing of multinational corporations, and so forth. While these approaches are good in themselves, they lack a broader vision that incorporates the necessity of moving beyond value production. Malott and Ford do not reject left liberal proposals such as these; they rather put them into a dialectical perspective. Since dialectics is about mediation and not the juxtaposition of binary oppositions, they see left liberal efforts at reform as important but limited when read against Marx's revolutionary call to transcend value production by building a communist future. In other words, it is not a question of "*either* reform *or* revolution" but rather "*both* reform *and* revolution." Yet it is important to stress that Malott and Ford put their fundamental emphasis on revolution. And that is what truly distinguishes their work from that of so many other left educational scholars, including many Marxists and neo-Marxists.

The authors write that the "necessary opulent consumption patterns of the simultaneously real and symbolic 1 percent situated next to the growing global immiseration of the vast majority increasingly reveals something inherently destructive and degrading about the process of creating and perpetually expanding capital." What it reveals, of course, is the logic of capital, a logic which the authors describe as "the very substance of capital's DNA, and it therefore cannot be reformed out of capital." So we don't need a genetically modified capitalism; what we need is a new gene pool of freely associated producers.

The authors address many pressing issues, including problematizing domestic and international colonized lands and the legacy of U.S. imperialism. Through this book, they push forward struggles against police brutality and murder, racism, sexism, patriarchy, and homophobia, connecting these struggles to economic bondage and to what they refer to, after Marx, as "personified capital," or the fashioning of bourgeois subjectivity. They incorporate into educational theory the framework of national oppression as a base for such organizing. Examining the means whereby the laws of commodity production (i.e., the exchange of equivalents) developed into the laws of capitalist accumulation, they uncover the myriad ways today in which these laws become ideologically mystified and, in so doing, uncover the "terrorist energy" identified by Marx that powers the dark engines of capital. More specific to the question of education, they reveal that "educational labor has a similar effect on the student as the machine has on the production of products," resulting in the creation of a class of passive dependents with no means to reproduce their existence outside of exchanging the value of their labor-power for a wage. They lucidly lay bare the hidden mechanisms of capitalist production relations as part of the pedagogical process of fostering revolutionary subjectivities antagonistic to capital.

Malott and Ford have undressed the educational formulae exercised by a neoliberal capitalism that has dramatically shifted investment from productive capital to money capital and that the authors argue must be deracinated:

> Financialization creates the appearance of growth, which may have no material basis. Rising profits in the financial sector do not necessarily come from real growth, but the plundering of public resources. In their quest for new markets and new sources of profit in an increasingly technicized world, the public sector has been a major target for hungry investors desperate to set capitals in motion to engage the process of expansion and accumulation. One strategy plays out something like this: taxes are reduced on the capitalist class; education is cut as state coffers dry up; the quality of said programs therefore becomes degraded; the public is thus more easily convinced that the problem with education, ironically, is that it lacks competition; privatization is proffered as the only solution.

Malott and Ford argue convincingly that the lineaments of the contemporary class struggle are best grasped through a historical examination of the *global class war*, and they utilize a framework developed by Sam Marcy in the 1950s that they persuasively argue "is more expansive and accurate than 'neoliberalism,' since it focuses on a conceptualization of global capitalist class strategy." This is an enormously timely and unique contribution to the field.

While Hollywood has glamorized the rotting corpse of industrial capital by rotating it toward a neo-Victorian steampunk postmodernism, layering the ruins of economic bondage with retro-futuristic fashions, architectures, and machines—effectively putting red leather goggles with brass fittings and leather shoulder and elbow armor decorated with clock parts on Marx's corpse—Malott and Ford do not succumb to theoretical fashion, even to admit that they are old fashioned. And given that scholars today have not yet caught up to Marx, they are old fashioned and at the same time decidedly ahead of their time. The result is a brilliant model of critical pedagogy based on Marx's *Critique of the Gotha Programme* and the work of Engels on the role of the state. As the authors proclaim:

The austerity measures ravaging much of the world make the most sense in the context of Engels's notion of the state as a "capitalist machine." The No Child Left Behind Act, Race to the Top, and the War on Terror in the United States are obvious products of this machine. Such insights challenge the rallying cries in critical pedagogy for saving public education from the neoliberal era's movement to privatize the welfare state by challenging the state itself as a mechanism and tool of capital. While public spaces tend to offer more room for creative critical pedagogies and, it might be argued, are therefore worth saving, today's capitalism cannot return to that of previous eras. What is more, the extreme right-wing political parties argue that public education is socialism and therefore must be freed from this monopoly so the most competitive products can rise to their market-determined place of superiority, allowing inferior competitors (i.e., schools) to perish. In this context, fighting for public education is a progressive position. For Marx, the state should fund education but have no control over its purpose or curriculum.

It is true, the authors warn, that critical pedagogy has for too long sojourned at the level of epistemology, and this must cease. And since we can't regulate capitalism out of existence, they propose an alternative that takes into account the social totality:

> In stark contrast to mainstream, domesticated currents that put critical pedagogy forward as a method of teaching and learning, we insist that critical pedagogy is part of a movement toward the radical transformation of the totality of social relations, which entails the *abolition* of capitalism and private-property–based social relations. This means—and this point is absolutely crucial—that our critical pedagogy is only interested in combating neoliberalism because neoliberalism is the current configuration of capitalism and the capital relation today. We are not interested in fighting neoliberal privatizations in the name of a kinder, gentler capitalism (which is always only kinder and gentler for some, of course). Or, more strategically speaking, we are interested in fighting neoliberalism insofar as that fight allows us to lay bare the fundamental logic of capital upon which it rests.

There is an urgency about the development of a critical pedagogy of becoming that follows this book onto every page and haunts our pedagogical imaginary. It can be best summarized in the authors' own words:

> This pedagogy of becoming is therefore not a casual call to action but comes with a sense of urgency that is not possible to exaggerate or overstate. Consequently, we might say that this critical pedagogy of becoming is intended to represent a rebellion in education. That is, this critical pedagogy is informed by the same insights informing Marx's hypothetical wage-workers, who uncover and become conscious of the fact that "wages are not what they *appear* to be, namely, the *value*, or *price*, *of labor*, but only a masked form for the *value*, or *price*, of *labor power*," and, as a result, develop

a full understanding of capitalism and become socialist organizers. Put another way, we might say that the goal of a Marxist critical pedagogy is to facilitate a class- and self-consciousness within students and teachers similar to that of the "…slaves who have at last got behind the secret of slavery and broken out in rebellion" (p. 15)… this critical pedagogy is so out of fashion at the present moment in the larger mainstream critical pedagogy community at the center of the capitalist power base, the United States, that Marxist educators often relate to Marx's dismay of how many socialists prescribed to the limited analysis showcased within the Gotha Programme.

The authors recognize that since Marxism does not examine historical realities irrespective of their specific contexts, Marx's works cannot be fixed in place and time or set in stone; in other words, Marxist theory serves as a means of bringing to light revolutionizing possibilities and potentialities from ever-shifting social realities and geopolitical contingencies. Marx did not supersede philosophy in favor of economic or political theory. To understand the relative expansion of capital in recurrently reshaping the globe as a series of geospacial investments and disinvestments requires that we understand the laws of tendency of capitalist production and the hegemonizing influence of education and work themselves. But it also demands that we acquire a philosophy of praxis. We can't transcend capitalism without first understanding its anatomy, its history, its evolutionary capacities. And understanding is a decidedly dialectical process, teasing out the internal relations of everyday life and the totality of social relations that inform it.

Critical pedagogy is a conduit to the universal on the part of the oppressed who work from their particular subjective formations and localities of struggle to transform the real, objective conditions of people's lives in the service of a nonalienated humanity engaged in freely associated labor. The authors describe it thusly as *"nonalienated humanity freely engaged in a planned, collective effort to reproduce social existence."* They go on to write:

> The Marxist dialectic allows us to understand that the potential to be free—to reunite thinking and doing—already exists within the alienated wageworker, from the privileged engineers and managers to the more oppressed manual laborers. Those of us who rely on a wage to survive are therefore contradictory—we embody our own potential negation as dehumanized existence because our vital powers, our humanness, are externally commanded and controlled.

The authors seek a social universe beyond value production, where we assimilate the tangible world as it assimilates us; where we are formed by the totality of the world in the search to meet the needs of our collective humanity; where the search for justice and our obligation to do justice become one and the same. This book should be read by all but especially those who are dependent wage laborers, those who have no other option but to sell their own labor-power for a price in order to obtain the use-values they need to reproduce themselves and the next generation of working-class laborers, laborers who will recursively toil for the capitalists, generation after generation, for the foreseeable future. But the future is becoming less and less foreseeable. To see the future and to struggle side by side for our existence demands that we recreate the future through our struggle. This requires that we follow Malott and Ford and go to the very limits of our humanity, that we plumb the abyss of the possible, and that we set ourselves upon the road of uncertainty to blaze a new communist trail into the unknown.

ACKNOWLEDGMENTS

Together we would first and foremost like to thank Peter McLaren for the rich body of Marxist critical pedagogy he has painstakingly produced, lived, and advocated for that gave inspiration and valuable insight into *Marx, Capital, and Education*. However odd it may seem, we must also thank Marx himself for the personal sacrifices he made expending his life's labor on charting the contours and trajectories of the capitalist mode of production, making pedagogical works like this possible. We are very grateful to Michael Peters and Peter McLaren for including this book in their cutting-edge Peter Lang series, Education and Struggle. Thanks also to Dave Hill, Brad Porfilio, and Colin Jenkins for publishing earlier versions of Chapters 1, 3, 4, and 5 in the *Journal for Critical Education Policy Studies*, *The SoJo Journal*, and *The Hampton Institute*. We would like to thank Chris Myers for generously facilitating the publication of this manuscript. Finally, we thank all of the workers helping to produce and distribute this book.

Curry would like to thank his wife, Donna, for her love, support, and feedback through the never-ending research and writing process. He would like to acknowledge his children, Jayne and Logan, for bringing true joy and hope to an otherwise intolerable bourgeois society. Curry would also like to thank his mother, Sally, his Aunt Sue, his sisters, Hannah and Kristen, all of his many cousins, nieces, aunts, uncles and family members for his foundation and grounding. A deep thanks are due to Derek for his unflinching and un-yielding communist contributions and collaboration; he is a true inspiration and leader in this project of *becoming*. Many thanks are also due to the West Chester University of Pennsylvania learning community, one of the last plac-es to contribute to critical pedagogy, being a publicly owned university. Curry also wants to express his deep respect and appreciation for all of his APSCUF (Association of Pennsylvania State College & University Faculties) comrades across the state of Pennsylvania. Finally, Curry would like to express his un-compromising solidarity with the critical pedagogy community the world over.

Derek would like to acknowledge his parents, Janet and Bob, and his grandmother, Beverly, for their unwavering support and encouragement. He would like to thank Curry for his comradeship, discipline, unbounded energy, and willingness to collaborate on this project. His advisor, Barbara Apple-baum, continues to provide crucial guidance, and his fellow graduate students in Cultural Foundations of Education at Syracuse University have provided a stimulating atmosphere, so thanks to Dave Wolken, Kelsey John, Mike Fraser, and Laura Jaffee. Many of the ideas presented in the book were born from struggling alongside his comrades in the ANSWER Coalition, THE General Body, Party for Socialism and Liberation, Revolutionary Communist Group, and global anti-imperialist movements more generally (Collin Chambers, Michael Kowalchuk, Maddie Horrell, Sarah Sloan, Richard Becker, Eugene Puryear, Brian Becker, Navid Nasr, Lizzie Phelan, Reverend Dexter, Marcel Cartier, Danny Shaw, Andrew Castro, and Carlos Martinez, to name a few). Sarah Pfohl's intellectual and pedagogical genius has proved infinitely influ-ential over the last few years. Finally, he couldn't imagine doing any of this without his companion species, Felix.

INTRODUCTION

"With communism as our horizon, the field of possibilities for revolutionary theory and practice starts to change shape. Barriers to action fall away. New potentials and challenges come to the fore. Anything is possible."

—JODI DEAN

Education is, by definition, a transformative process. When one enters into an educational engagement—knowingly or unknowingly—one is necessarily changed in some way. At the very least, the information that one knows is altered in some form or manner. At the other extreme, and still at the level of the individual, one's very subjectivity is reconstituted. The stakes become even greater when we look at education at the scale of society. Indeed, to say that education has the power to transform society or the world borders on the mundane. We would be hard pressed, for example, to name one contemporary leading political figure that did not resort to such clichés. Yet our problem with such proclamations is not that they are banal but that they are completely devoid of direction. The content, nature and, most importantly, the direction and potentiality of this transformation are completely immaterial to education itself. In other words, yes, education can change people and societies, but *how* and—just as importantly—*toward what ends?*[1]

It is these questions in which this book intervenes. We are, to be sure, not merely concerned with raising and exploring these questions because they are interesting or provide for good academic inquiry. We are concerned rather with beginning to answer them, and we pursue this task in an unapologetically partisan manner. That is, we are most interested in investigating the movement toward communism and the role that critical pedagogy can play in this transition. A large part of this endeavor entails a critical understanding of the past and the present, an excavation of the underlying logics and often-opaque forces that have—and continue to—determine the world-historic context in which we find ourselves, and out of which we struggle to teach, learn, study, and act ourselves. As any good militant knows, a proper grasp of the historical and contemporary contours of life is paramount to formulating and enacting courses of action and forms of organization that effectively contribute to the production of counterpower. Possible futures, after all, do not materialize out of nowhere; they are always only immanent in the present.

Even more than being vacuous, to call for change and transformation from within capitalism can be, in a strange way, to call for more of the same. This is so because capitalism is an incredibly dynamic system that must always be in motion. When, for example, the circulation of a particular commodity ceases for whatever reason, that commodity becomes literally valueless. It is for this reason that there is nothing so traumatizing for a merchant capitalist as a warehouse full of commodities with nowhere to go or for a money capitalist as a bank with no deposits or withdrawals or for a productive capitalist as a machine or worker sitting idle. Capitalism is defined by rapid motion, by the permanent "revolutionising [of] the instruments of production, and thereby the relations of production, and with them the whole relations of society" (Marx and Engels, 1848/1972, p. 476).

This perpetual process of transformation has produced us as subjects who not only are open to change, but actually demand it. Marshall Berman (1982/1988) writes about this phenomenon, noting that "for people, whatever their class, to survive in modern society, their personalities must take on the fluid and open form of this society" (p. 95). However, if people are used to—and indeed desire—constant change, then how can they be expected to endlessly conform to the roles assigned to them by bourgeois society? Here we encounter a limit that capitalism must continually negotiate, and the way in which this limit has most effectively been managed has been to produce a circumscribed field of the possible. Nearly anything goes so long as the political-economic order based on the rule of private property goes unchallenged.

In order for education to contribute to the generation of a counterpower, it has to place capital squarely in its crosshairs. More than that, it has to open up the field of possibilities, enabling the imagination of a world without the exploitation and oppression that characterizes capital. The reader will therefore not find any vague talk in this book about "inclusion," "making society more just," "expanding or reclaiming the public sphere," or "restraining dominant power." In fact, one will not even read of "democracy." While we are not opposed to any of the former terms, in an effort to contribute to the tearing open of the field of the possible beyond the limits imposed on it by bourgeois forms of thought, we write about communism. In doing so, we join a growing chorus of voices on the Left who have begun to mobilize our insurgent outrage and desire under the banner of communism.

Communism, for us, best captures the simultaneously beautiful and tragic, inspiring and frustrating history of the international proletarian struggle that we inherit and inhabit. We cannot divorce ourselves from the course of the actually existing workers' struggle as it has undulated, particularly since its eruption on the world scene with the Bolshevik Revolution in 1917. To attempt to divorce ourselves from this lineage would be to withdraw from politics altogether and forfeit the possibility of moving beyond capitalism; communism remains the alternative to capitalism. To be sure, we inhabit this history critically, acknowledging its victories and accomplishments as well as its tragedies and errors. But we make no apologies.

Out of all of the radical scholars that have returned to communism in the last decade, Jodi Dean's (2012) theorization of communism as a "horizon" is particularly helpful for framing contemporary political struggles. A horizon announces an absolute division. The earth's horizon, for example, separates off those lines of visibility that converge with the ground and those that dissipate into the sky. The communist horizon is thus the political division in which we are constituted; it "impresses upon us the necessity to abolish capitalism and to create global practices and institutions of egalitarian cooperation" (p. 6). Importantly, Dean's (2012) use of the term "communism" is not synonymous with "democracy," as it is for others, like Michael Hardt and Antonio Negri. Communism, in its insistence on division, stands opposed to democracy, which "avoids the fundamental antagonism between the 1 percent and the rest of us by acting as if the only thing really missing was participation" (pp. 57–58).

All of this is well and good, it might be objected, but does it really make strategic sense to call ourselves communists now, given the history of anti-communism in the U.S. and its absolute conflation with "totalitarianism" or "authoritarianism?" We have several responses to this. The first response is that revolutions are not popularity contests, and appeals to what is popular result in the sacrificing of principles and concessions to bourgeois ideology. Thus, when we make excuses for being communists, or when we instead refer to ourselves as "radical democrats" or some other platitude, we actually work to reinforce anti-worker ideology and obscure the class struggle. Further, we assume in advance that we are only talking to a select group of people. For masses of workers and oppressed people across the globe, communism does not conjure up images of uniformity, dullness, and rationality but of international solidarity and victorious anti-colonial liberation struggles. The second response is that recent protests, insurrections, and revolutions across the globe have placed communism back on the table as not only a viable but, moreover, a desirable alternative to the injustice and exploitation that define neoliberal capitalism (and capitalism more generally). The third response is that, even if we were to take all of the negative (and mostly incorrect) associations that people have with communism, these would still pale in comparison to the astonishing violence and genocides carried out in the name of democracy. Rather than shying away from the term "communism" and taking cover in democracy, we confront head-on the ideological distortions that have permeated U.S. society and other capitalist democracies.

Communism, of course, is not some objective, static state. Quite the opposite. In fact, at one point in his *Grundrisse* notebooks, Marx (1939/1973) writes that communism is "the absolute movement of becoming" (p. 488). This movement of becoming dialectically links the subjective and the objective, and it is in this way that we focus on education as a process of becoming. In other words, the critical pedagogy that we develop in the following pages recognizes both that subjectivity takes shape within—and as a result of—the totality of capital *and* that it is, in the last instance, subjects that push against and, hopefully, beyond that totality. As such, the ways in which we understand ourselves and our world are of the utmost importance. As an example, one would be extremely hard pressed to find someone who does not know another, or at least has heard of another, who is struggling financially because of what are perceived to be *bad life choices*, such as dropping out of school; having too many children at too young an age; over spending beyond one's means; making unwise decisions regarding one's romantic life; being an insubordinate employee and getting fired; abusing drugs and alcohol; etc. With a psychologized and decontextualized dominant bourgeois ideology in place, it is not hard to convince working people to view our own poverty as the product of irresponsible behavior rather than a consequence of the historical development of capital and its internal logic that is mediated through the agency of antagonistic social classes. We need a critical pedagogy that can help us discern the processes at work below the surface of poverty, the underlying structures and forces that coordinate our lives; one that, in so doing, transforms not only our consciousness but our very being.

The task of the critical educator, then, is to understand the present determinations of our time, to begin to imagine and orient ourselves toward the communist future, and propose and engage in a process by which we might become into that future. As teachers, organizers, and activists, we are principally concerned with the ways in which education is a central component in the reproduction of exploitation and oppression and the ways in which it can become central to the communist struggle and a communist future. In exploring this question, we have drawn heavily upon revolutionary critical pedagogy—which is something of a synthesis of critical pedagogy and Marxist educational theory—and especially the work of Peter McLaren. Due in no small part to the heightening of contradictions of global capital—expressed succinctly in the rhetoric of the 1% versus the 99%—there has been a renewed interest in both Marxist educational theory and critical pedagogy. What is most politically promising for revolutionary educators in this renewal is the potential to bridge the two fields. This is particularly important for critical pedagogy, as this field has gradually become domesticated within academic institutions and teacher training programs, being reduced to a "method" of dialogue or an approach to navigating the teacher-student relationship. The conversation is also important for Marxist educational theory, because critical pedagogy places particular emphasis on the ways in which classrooms and schools relate to, impact, and are determined by broader social and political forces.

As a body of literature and praxis, critical pedagogy has historically been oriented toward intervening in and transforming exploitative and oppressive social relations. Early iterations of critical pedagogy, such as the one articulated in Henry Giroux's (1983) classic *Theory & Resistance in Education*, were thus focused heavily on *revealing* systems of oppression and exploitation, of demonstrating the systemic and interconnected mechanisms operating behind the backs of the oppressed. One of Freire's great contributions—and one that, unfortunately, has overshadowed his many others—is the dialogical and creative means by which this takes place. This first phase of critical pedagogy relies heavily upon the Critical Theory of the Frankfurt School, as represented by thinkers such as Theodor Adorno, Max Horkheimer, Herbert Marcuse, and, to a lesser extent, Walter Benjamin. Responding to what they saw as the economic determinism of the Third International and official socialism, the Frankfurt School project represented an attempt to subject the superstructure of capitalist society to a rigorous critique. As Giroux (1983) notes, "while orthodox Marxist theory established a relationship between culture and the material forces of society, it did so by reducing culture to a mere reflex of the economic realm" (p. 22). Attempting to combat the trend of economic determinism, the Frankfurt School emphasized the superstructural elements of society and the role that elements such as culture, knowledge, language, and desire play in the maintenance and reproduction of oppression, inequality, and injustice (i.e., capitalist social relations). Many of these elements, such as knowledge and language, are of course intimately connected with schooling and education, which led Peter McLaren (1985), for example, when outlining the major concepts utilized in critical pedagogy, to write about such concepts as ideology, hegemony, cultural capital, and discourse.

The late 1980s and 1990s saw a radical proliferation of critical pedagogies, many of which were influenced by the then-burgeoning fields of post-structuralism and feminism. This was an intense period of debate about and within the field of critical pedagogy concerning issues of power and teacher authority, rationality and irrationality, dialogue and voice, and the relationship between knowledge and the "truth." There were important insights generated and contradictions revealed in these debates, although many of the critics, such as Patti Lather and Elizabeth Ellsworth, did not engage in a sustained conversation and critique. Thus, at the end of the 20th century, there was a definite dip in the generation of critical pedagogical thought. This was also accompanied by a mainstreaming of critical pedagogy, a packaging of critical pedagogy, and its reduction to "dialogue" and "student-teacher/teacher-student" practice.

Recently, however, we have witnessed a resurgence of critical pedagogy and a shift away from the debates of the 1990s and toward a sustained critique of educational privatizations and, more generally, neoliberalism. A new wave of scholars, far too numerous to name, has provided integral analyses of the contemporary phase of capitalism, its impact on schools, students, teachers, and educational processes, and ways that these impacts are being channeled. These insights have been bolstered by the work of Henry Giroux and others. Additionally, we are currently witnessing a resurgence of Marxist theorizing in critical education and critical pedagogy. This recent turn, including scholars from around the world, has centered the capital-labor relation and the class dialectic as a central concern. We believe that critiques of neoliberalism and educational privatizations must be seen in context with this latter work, enabling the former trends to be located within an overarching framework of capitalist exploitation and oppression.

As a contribution to revolutionary critical pedagogy, this book is based on a systematic and educational reading of a variety of Marx's works. Two principal texts are Marx's Paris manuscripts, published posthumously as *Economic and Philosophic Manuscripts of 1844*, and the first volume of *Capital*. We also rely on the *Critique of the Gotha Programme* and volumes two and three of *Capital*. It is clear that we do not read a "young" Marx against a "mature" Marx.[2] We stick fairly close to Marx throughout this book and do not get too sidetracked into the debates in the secondary literature.[3]

The book proceeds in several steps. In the first chapter, we present the way in which we understand the process of becoming. In order to cultivate this notion, we turn to Marx's early philosophical work and concentrate in particular on his appropriation and re-contextualization of Hegel's dialectics. While Hegel saw becoming as the process through which abstract or divine ideals were achieved in practice, for Marx, the process of becoming concerns the metabolic relationship between humans and nature, a liberated humanism, which we also refer to as the *production of the system of nature*. We acknowledge the tension that humanism has historically caused within the Marxist theoretical and political tradition. It is certainly true that a particular conception of humanism was deployed to justify the right-wing shift of the international communist movement that began in the 1950s. This was a humanism that obscured the fundamental class antagonism that runs throughout society by replacing the category of "class" with that of "man" (Althusser, 1971/2008). This anti-Marxist humanism certainly had a deleterious effect on the global class struggle, particularly as it influenced the domestic and international policies of the Soviet Union. Sam Marcy (1990), for instance, cites a 1988 speech given by Mikhail Gorbachev to the United Nations General Assembly, in which he did not speak once about workers or classes but about "universal human values" and "universal ideas." Marcy correctly notes that there "never has been any consensus on what universal human interests are. Each class and each social grouping evaluates human interests from its own point of view" (p. 31). We refer to a class-based humanism in the hopes that the human can engage in a process of becoming, and in this way we also gesture toward the important ecopedagogical work being done against anthropocentrism (e.g., Kahn, 2010).

Negation is key to the process of becoming because it harnesses the contradictions of the present, turning a phenomenon—like private property—into its opposite. This act, however, is not enough, for at this stage, the act of negation has not yet freed itself from the contradiction. This is why the negation of the negation, or absolute negativity, is required. Through this process, the "negation establishes a relation with itself" (McLaren, 2015, p. 17), liberating itself from prior determinants. To connect the negation of the negation to the contemporary crisis of education in capitalism, we shift to Marx's changing conception of the tendency for the rate of profit to fall. We look to this particular contradiction to examine how we might negate ourselves as alienated labor-power, reclaiming our labor-power, and, through another act of negation, liberating our labor from labor-power.[4]

The second chapter moves to an examination of the current political and economic situation. There seems to be a consensus in critical educational studies and on the left more generally that the contemporary political-economic moment is best defined as "neoliberal." We claim that neoliberalism is a necessary but ultimately insufficient framework for understanding the contemporary contours of the class struggle. We argue, contra David Harvey, that neoliberalism is part of a global capitalist class strategy and not merely a class strategy *within* capitalism. To make this argument, we deploy the framework of the global class war, developed in the 1950s by Sam Marcy. This framework locates the "capital-labor" compromise that occurred within capitalist countries in the post-World War II era as part of a more general and global working-class offensive, thereby linking developments in capitalist countries with the world-historic socialist and national liberation movements that swept the globe throughout much of the 20th century. We are now enduring a period of global counterrevolution, and we demonstrate that neoliberalism is a part of this counterrevolutionary strategy. We pay special attention to China, offering a more nuanced and class-conscious conception of China's Communist Party and the socialist potential it continues to possess, which serves as a corrective to Harvey's interpretation. At the end of the chapter, we offer some concluding comments on how this framework contributes to our critical pedagogy of becoming, using the 2011 U.S. war on Libya as an example.[5]

Having established a framework that accounts for the contemporary determinants of the world situation in which critical pedagogy operates, in the third chapter, we turn our attention to imagining a communist future and ways that we might work toward that future. In order to do this, we perform an educational reading of Marx's *Critique of The Gotha Programme*. In this text, Marx outlines specific steps that can be taken in the fight for socialism and communism. As historical-materialists, we do not look to this text as a blueprint for our own future, as it was written in and for a different historical moment. We read the text programmatically, looking at the historical content, relevant points of antagonism with social democrats, and overall purpose of the text. In order to do this, we situate this work within the overall body of thought and work of Marx and Engels. At the end of the chapter, we draw out six elements of critical pedagogy of becoming, including a recognition and rejection of anti-communism; an orientation toward the totality of life; an insistence on the connection to global struggles against exploitation and oppression (which includes an evaluation of the class character of these struggles); the utilization of critical, rigorous concepts and formulations; the location of our project within the communist horizon; and the necessity of organization and the Party.

In the fourth chapter, we continue to flesh out the process of becoming by calling on Marx's reading of the ways in which the era of manufacture developed into the more technically complex industrial era through the advancement of machinery. What this discussion points to is how the internal logic of capital drives it toward not only more technically extensive instruments of production but that those instruments of production are designed to lead to growing economic exploitation and intellectual alienation and degradation. It is this tendency that necessitates the birth of "modern" (i.e., formal and standardized) education, and we locate No Child Left Behind and the Common Core Standards Movement within this larger trajectory of the capital-labor relation. Homing in on the current state of social studies education, we develop a Revolutionary Marxist Social Studies program that offers students the intellectual tools needed to demystify bourgeois ideology and discover and resist the hidden process of value augmentation. And here we should address the terrible misunderstanding about the process of demystification that has animated so many critiques of critical pedagogy (e.g., Biesta, 1998; Burbules and Berk, 1999). Demystification is not about revealing the truth about something that was previously mystifying and therefore false. Antonio Negri (2014) presents three reasons why such an understanding is incorrect. First, in Marxism, these are *economic* and not abstract categories. Second, mystifications can indeed be true in the sense that we live and breathe them and that they in many ways can define the parameters of our being. Third, "the process of demystification is none other than the revelation of the [class] interests behind an affirmation" (pp. 279–280).

We next connect our critical pedagogy of becoming to the streets and in particular the anti-police brutality resistance movement that erupted like a wildfire in late 2014. Our intervention in this chapter is intended to contribute to the anti-capitalist elements circulating within this movement. This effort requires us to focus on the relationship between race and class in the U.S. To say that the deadly effects of white supremacy, racism, and the criminalization and ultimately erasure of Black life in the U.S. can be traced back to the long legacy of anti-Blackness that was central to the justification of slavery is an important but incomplete insight. The vicious and dehumanizing racism advanced by European slavers, we show, became deadly when cotton became an international commodity, thereby propelling slavery from a system designed to produce local use-values to one designed to produce international exchange-values. Capitalism, this analysis suggests, continues to be the force driving the deadliness of white supremacy in the contemporary context. The emergence of Historically Black Colleges and Universities is located with the transition from slavery to wage labor, and we pay attention to the historical and contemporary progressive and revolutionary role played by such institutions. At the end of the chapter, we call on the concept of national oppression—and its history in the international communist movement—as an important way to mobilize against racialized capitalist exploitation. To do this, we turn to the largely unappreciated theoretical and political work of Harry Haywood.

In the final chapter, we return to the theme of subjectivity and our contention that we pay particular attention to the structural and systemic co-ordinates within and through which our subjectivities are fashioned and re-fashioned. But here we focus on the subjectivity of capital, or the capitalist, which Marx referred to as "capital personified." We examine the historical development of the figure of the capitalist as determined by the coercive laws of competition. This not only provides additional evidence to the fact that the most degrading and destructive aspects of capitalism cannot be reformed out of it but must instead be overthrown; it also allows us to argue that the capitalist has no right to exist, at least not *qua* capitalist. This is perhaps one of the most crucial yet neglected ideas in Freire's (1970/1998) *Pedagogy of the Oppressed*: repression has an important role to play in the process of liberation.

What follows is a contribution to revolutionary critical pedagogy. As militant teachers and organizers, we offer this book as a weapon to others in the struggle against capital. We make no pretensions as to offering a comprehensive or complete vision or program; indeed, these are always the result of the organized masses in motion. We instead hope to start a sustained conversation about the praxis needed to wage a proletarian offensive in the global class war; how we can continue teaching, learning, studying, and acting ourselves into a new mode of production; how we can ultimately overthrow the existing order and institute a new set of social relations that for the first time truly enables the *becoming* of humanity to take place.

Notes

1. Gert Biesta (2010) makes a similar argument about the language of learning that dominates contemporary educational discourse. In addition to being an individualistic concept, he writes, "'learning' is basically a *process* term. It denotes process and activity but is open—if not empty—with regard to content and direction" (p. 18).
2. This is not intended as a repetition of the now customary dig at Althusser. Indeed, we acknowledge that the political climate in which Althusser was operating provided justifiable grounds for his formulation of Marx's epistemological break.
3. For those interested in a synthesis of many of these debates, we recommend David Harvey's (1982/2006) *Limits to Capital*.
4. The distinction between labor, as a necessary process through which we produce ourselves and the world, and labor-power, the expropriation and alienation of that process under capitalism, is necessary to our argument. It is the inability to understand this distinction that leads David Geoffrey Smith (2009) to critique Peter McLaren and Paula Allman by writing that "the human condition cannot be delivered from the necessity of labor itself" (p. 113); Smith conflates labor and labor-power.
5. Note that we use "critical pedagogy of becoming" and "Marxist pedagogy of becoming" interchangeably throughout the book.

· 1 ·

BECOMING THROUGH NEGATION:
REVISITING MARX'S HUMANISM

Introduction

In this chapter, we begin the process of developing a Marxist critical pedagogy of becoming by turning to Marx's approach to Hegelian dialectics. We begin with a brief outline of Marx's take on Hegel's dialectics. Because of the current crisis of capital, we look to Marx's shifting conception of the falling rate of profit (which reflects his developing understanding of how contradictions operate within capitalism). We argue that this analysis reflects Marx's developing understanding of what the negation of the negation means under capitalism. Due to the role that the United States continues to play as the center of global capitalism, these discussions focus on the U.S. We might note, drawing on Hegelian dialectics, that the hegemonic logic of capital serves the purpose of preventing the tendency of capital's contradictions from leading to social transformation, or revolution. We argue throughout the chapter that critical pedagogy can offer a powerful tool in helping students and teachers situate their own experiences in this larger social, historical context, fostering self-empowerment and collective critical agency. In other words, in order to negate ourselves as alienated labor, we need to be able to see ourselves as such, see ourselves as the negation of ourselves as such, and, finally, engage in the negation ourselves. For Marx, as we will see below, this is the historical process of becoming, which, in line with Paulo Freire, should be conceived of as a never-ending process, one that is rigorously lived, both individually and collectively. The nature of existence here is conceptualized as perpetual movement. As we noted in the introduction, the question is: in what direction shall this movement proceed? Bringing these questions to the surface and challenging students and teachers to think deeply and seriously about what it means to answer them is the task of critical pedagogy.

Revisiting Hegelian Dialectics

The North American turn away from Marxist analysis in educational theory following the symbolic fall of the Berlin Wall and the advent of postmodern theory would lead critical pedagogy down the road of liberalism—a road dominated by identity politics and a Weberian conception of social class (McLaren, 2005). Building a new approach to Marxist educational theory for the twenty-first century in North America and beyond, Peter McLaren has transcended the crude economic determinism and limited understanding of Marx within North American education circles prevalent in the 1970s. In the process of developing this groundbreaking critical pedagogy, McLaren has introduced the critical pedagogy community to cutting-edge Marxist philosophers such as Peter Hudis (2012), who has gone to great lengths to flesh out and celebrate Marx's concept of the alternative to capitalism and its connection to Hegelian dialectics, which could not be more relevant to a Marxist critical pedagogy.

Hudis (2012) argues that traditional Marxism is based on the false assumption that Marx rejected Hegel's dialectics for its idealism. Rather, Hudis demonstrates that Marx does not in fact reject Hegel's dialectics but revises it. In so doing, Marx (1844/1988) argues that "there is a double error in Hegel" (p. 147). The first error is that while Hegel understood the essence of man/woman as the outcome of his/her own labor, he wrongly took consciousness, rather than material conditions, as absolute reality:

> …Wealth, state-power, etc. are understood by Hegel as entities estranged from the *human* being, this only happens in their form as thoughts…They are thought-entities, and therefore an estrangement of *pure* i.e., abstract, philosophical thinking… The whole *history of the alienation-process* and the whole *process of the retraction* of the alienation is therefore nothing but the *history of the production* of abstract (i.e. absolute) thought—of logical, speculative thought. (p. 147)

Hudis (2012) summarizes Marx's critique of Hegel here as involving the inversion of what Marx calls the subject and object. Correcting this, Marx argues that it is not the opposition between consciousness and self-consciousness that needs to be overcome but the opposition between "abstract thinking and sensuous reality" (p. 148). For Hegel, then, "the appropriation of man's essential powers, which have become objects—indeed alien objects—is thus in the *first place* only an *appropriation* occurring in *consciousness*, in *pure thought*—i.e., in *abstraction*: it is the appropriation of these objects as *thoughts* and *movements of thought*" (Marx, 1844/1988, p. 148). These sections of Marx's *1844 Manuscripts* have been used to justify the position that Marx flipped Hegel right side up, placing him back on Earth on his feet and rejecting his core philosophy in the process. Challenging this reading, Hudis (2012) is struck by how Marx's next few passages have been largely missed or ignored, even by self-proclaimed Marxists:

> But inasmuch as it keeps steadily in view man's *estrangement*, even though man appears only in the shape of mind, there lie concealed in it *all* the elements of criticism, already *prepared* and *elaborated* in a manner often rising far above the Hegelian standpoint...The outstanding thing in Hegel...is...the dialectic of negativity as the moving and generating principle. (pp. 148–149)

Clearly, Marx is not exactly "breaking" from Hegel in this moment. Rather than abandoning Hegel, Marx is re-contextualizing his dialectics, his negation of the negation. As an example, it would be best to turn momentarily to a sizable excerpt from Hegel (1812/1993) himself. In the following quote, we find the philosophical kernels that Marx both critiqued and praised:

> The absolute itself appears only as the negation of all predicates and as the void. But since equally it must be pronounced as the position of all predicates, it appears as the most formal contradiction...The absolute is not merely being, nor even essence... The identity of the absolute is thus the absolute identity, since each of its parts is itself the whole, or each determinateness is the totality, that is, determinateness as such has become an utterly transparent illusory being, a difference which has vanished in its positedness. Essence, existence, the world-in-itself, whole, parts, force—these reflected determinations appear to ordinary thinking as a true being which is valid in and for itself; but the absolute as against them is the ground in which they have been engulfed...The absolute does not determine itself; for determination is a form difference which, in the first instance, counts as such...In the absolute itself is no becoming, for it is not being...It is the beyond of the manifold differences and determinations and their movement, a beyond which *lies at the back of the absolute*;

consequently, though it accepts them, it also destroys them; it is thus the *negative exposition* of the absolute...The logical movement of the sphere of *being and essence*, the content of which has not yet been raked together from outside as something given and contingent, or submerged in the abyss of the absolute by a reflection alien to that content...But at the same time this exposition has itself a *positive* side; for in so far as in it the finite fall to the ground, it demonstrates that its nature is to be connected with the absolute, or to contain the absolute within itself... (pp. 530–533)

The dialectical movement expressed here, taken from the first chapter (The Absolute) of the final section (Actuality) of *Logic*, constitutes a good portion of the brilliance Marx saw within Hegel's work. Hegel is pointing to what would be interpreted by Marx as a structurally determined movement toward the end of capital and simultaneously toward the emergence of something new, something absolutely distinct from *what is*. Significantly elaborating on these essential contributions he saw within Hegel, Marx (1844/1988) writes:

Hegel conceives the self-genesis of man as a process, conceives objectification as loss of the object, as alienation and as transcendence of this alienation; that he thus grasps the essence of *labor* and comprehends objective man—true, because real man—as the outcome of man's *own labor*...Hegel's standpoint is that of modern political economy. He grasps *labor* as the *essence* of man—as man's essence in the act of proving itself: he sees only the positive, not the negative side of labor. Labor is man's *coming-to-be for himself* within *alienation*, or as *alienated* man. The only labor which Hegel knows and recognizes is *abstractly mental* labor...For Hegel the *essence of man—man*—equals *self-consciousness*. All estrangement of the human essence is therefore *nothing but estrangement of self-consciousness*. The estrangement of self-consciousness is not regarded as an *expression of the real* estrangement of the human being—its expression reflected in the realm of knowledge and thought. Instead, the *real* estrangement—that which appears real—is from its *innermost*, hidden nature (a nature only brought to light by philosophy) nothing but the *manifestation* of the estrangement of the real essence of man, of *self-consciousness*...The man who takes hold of his essential being is *merely* the self-consciousness which takes hold of objective essences. Return of the object into the self is therefore the re-appropriation of the object. (pp. 149–151)

Again, even in his affirmation of Hegel, Marx's correction can be found in all of its rigor and vitality: essence is more than consciousness, and thus the transcendence of estrangement is more than a mere mental act. As we will see, this is fundamental for correcting a growing tendency in critical pedagogy that reduces liberation to the self-reflective process of acquiring a critical consciousness as an end in itself (rather than a prerequisite for fostering a collective approach and targeting a more material or concrete object of intervention). At the same time, Marx is not necessarily arguing for a form of *materialism over idealism* but for an alternative to this dichotomy, what he calls *humanism* or *naturalism*:

> Here we see how consistent naturalism or humanism distinguishes itself both from idealism and materialism, constituting at the same time the unifying truth of both. We see also how only naturalism is capable of comprehending the act of world history. (p. 154)

Naturalism, as opposed to the abstractness of idealism, is grounded in the fact that humans are sensuous beings that are *in* and *of* the natural, concrete world and thus endowed with "natural powers of life" (p. 154) that compel and drive us. The species' natural, biological endowments simultaneously enable and limit the human life as it engages objects external to it—"objects of his *need*—essential *objects*, indispensible to the manifestation and confirmation of his essential powers" (p. 154). Using hunger as an example, Marx notes that, "*hunger* is a natural *need*; it therefore needs a *nature* outside itself, an *object* outside itself, in order to satisfy itself, to be stilled" (p. 154). Contrasting this concreteness to what we might take as the abstractness of absolute knowledge read, in the most progressive sense, as self-consciousness, which displaces the object for the idea of the object, Marx notes that "a being which does not have its nature outside itself is not a *natural* being, and plays no part in the system of nature" (pp. 154–155). Transitioning to the uniqueness of human history, Marx makes the point that because humans are objective and sensuous beings, they suffer, and because humans feel what they suffer, they are *passionate* beings. Consequently, "passion is the essential force of man energetically bent on its object" (p. 155).

Before proceeding, we wish to emphasize that there is not a sharp binary between the human and nature. Indeed, as early as 1845, Marx and Engels (1845/1970) noted in their critique of Feuerbach that "nature, the nature that preceded human history... is nature which today no longer exists anywhere" (p. 63). This is not to say that humans have mastered nature in any way, as recent environmental crises clearly demonstrate. It is rather to say, as Neil Smith (1984/2008) has convincingly demonstrated, that nature is produced. Even human nature is produced: "The development of the hand, from a means of locomotion into a sophisticated limb for the manipulation of tools, is accomplished gradually by thousands of years of labor" (p. 56). In other words, nature is the product of labor. Under capitalism, the production of nature is revolutionized in that "for the first time human beings produce nature at a world scale" (p. 77); "No part of the earth's surface, the atmosphere, the oceans, the geological substratum, or the biological superstratum [that] are immune from transformation by capital" (p. 79).

We find confirmation of our reading of humanism in Marx by turning to biographic details provided by Marx's youngest daughter, Eleanor Marx Aveling (1896/2014), in the introduction to a series of articles on Revolution and Counter-Revolution in 1848 Germany. Ironically, these unsuccessful peasant rebellions (i.e., the counter revolutions) would lead to Marx's expulsion from Germany and then France and ultimately to his refuge in London. To best understand his work, the reader would benefit from knowing the details of "the conditions under which [he] was working" (p. 5). When Marx speaks of suffering and passion, despite his *middle-class* background, he is speaking from experience.

Being a refugee, for Marx—like millions of refugees—is not experienced alone. First, refugees, like immigrants more generally, don't emerge as individuals but are born of historic changes as societies develop new modes of production or undergo other economic, political, or social transformations. Consequently, refugees are part of a community of refugees. Many of these people are parents. Marx was a husband and a parent. Consequently, when he found refuge in London and was "more or less destitute," experiencing "years of horrible poverty" and "bitter suffering" (p. 5), he did so from the perspective of a parent who lost a number of children along the way. Describing one of these horrific and deeply saddening losses experienced by the Marx family, Aveling Marx quotes from her mother's notes: "three days…the poor child wrestled with death. She suffered so…Her little dead body lay in the small back room… We wept for the little angel resting near us, cold and dead. The death of the dear child came in the time of our bitterest poverty. Our German friends could not help us…" (p. 6). When Marx speaks of suffering and passion, it is a knowledge gained not just from rigorous study and critique—however indispensable these forms of inquiry are—but also from his lived, *sensuous* experience.

Showing her readers an image of Marx as the passionate father toiling away on some of the world's most important manuscripts, Marx Aveling writes, "in that 'front room' in Dean Street, the children playing about him, Marx worked. I have heard tell how the children would pile up chairs behind him to represent a coach, to which he was harnessed as horse, and would 'whip him up' even as he sat at his desk writing" (pp. 6–7). Supporting this sentiment, that Marx was not *just* a fiery writer and revolutionary, but a deeply caring and engaged father, Jonathan Sperber (2013), in his acclaimed biography, *Karl Marx: A Nineteenth Century Life*, argues that, "the desolate moods that followed his children's death bespoke a paternal love that was anything but distant. Marx profoundly enjoyed the presence of children" (p. 469). Sperber cites Wilhelm Liebknecht, who spent much time with Marx at his home: "one must have seen Marx with his children to obtain a complete notion of the depths of sentiment and the childlike nature of this hero of *Wissenschaft*. In his free minutes, or while strolling, he brought them along, played the wildest and most lively games with them—in short he was a child among children" (p. 469). From these works and reflections on Marx, we get a picture of Karl as a passionate father and lover of life, someone who deeply understood the human condition and the great joy that can be found within living. In other words, we might play with Marx's own words and note that he was a person concretely connected to *the system of nature* (a system that, again, is not separate from but is instead a product of labor and, under capitalism, labor-power).

Being able to see the deep connections between Marx the writer and Marx the human being is invaluable, particularly for those of us engaged in education. In this context, his work finds remarkable vitality and relevance. For example, connecting his discussions on the passion and sensuousness of the human being—as a counter to Hegel's abstractness—to his developing humanism is insightful. That is, Marx (1844/1988) was clear that the human is not merely a natural being but a *human* natural being and "a being for himself," that is, a "species being who has to confirm and manifest himself as such both in his being and in his knowing" (p. 155). Uniting being and knowing here, Marx brings us back to his previous statement that humanism is both epistemological and ontological. In other words, humans not only require knowledge of self but the material conditions necessary for the collective human society to develop its natural, human capacities, which Hegel described as *becoming*. However, as we will see below, becoming for Hegel was about realizing an abstract, divine essence and was limited to the realm of pure thought. Bringing the reader back to his other point that humanism is the basis for history, Marx comments:

> ...*Human* objects are not natural objects as they immediately present themselves, and neither is *human sense* as it immediately *is*—as it is objectively—*human* sensibility, human objectivity. Neither nature objectively nor nature subjectively is directly given in a form adequate to the human being. And as everything natural has to have its beginning, man too has his act of coming-to-be—history—which, however, is for him a known history, and hence as an act of coming-to-be it is a conscious

self-transcending act of coming-to-be. History is the true natural history of man. (pp. 155–156)

We might again remind ourselves that what Marx is capturing here is the culmination of his correction of Hegel's dialectical movement. The ontological and epistemological perspective here is the heart of Freire's critical pedagogy and continues to be the focus of the critical pedagogy tradition, especially the Marxist approach developed by Peter McLaren, Dave Hill, Glenn Rikowski, Paula Allman, Antonia Darder, Rich Gibson, and others. Ontologically, the world is conceived of as a process and continuously in motion. It is a concrete world driven by concrete human needs—needs that transform and develop as we make and remake our world. The ability or inability of humanity being a part of this process determines, to a large extent, the level of self-actualization and "coming-to-be" in a given mode of production and historical era. Epistemologically, Marx helps us here direct the knowledge production process through education. That is, the purpose of a critical education is to overcome the ideological and material obstacles of "coming-to-be." Marx offers a concrete, historical context to understand this uniquely human process.

Transformation through Negation

While Marx's development of the dialectic is growing in complexity and clarity, his challenge to Hegel is not yet complete. That is, by reducing the sensuous world to pure thought, Hegel winds up reaffirming estrangement rather than transcending it, as his negation of the negation implies. In this respect, Marx (1844/1988) accuses Hegel's *positive* (i.e., a new beginning), that exists within the negative (i.e., the world as it exists), of being a "false positive" because it "pretends to be *at home in his other-being as such*" (p. 158). Expressing Hegel's logic here in its most general terms, Marx describes it in the following way, "reason is at home in unreason as unreason" (p. 158). As an example, Marx refers to "the man who has recognized that he is leading an alienated life in politics, law, etc., is leading his true life in this alienated life as such" (p. 158). A heavy blow is then delivered to Hegel: "with him the negation of the negation is the confirmation of the pseudo-essence, or of the self-estranged essence in its denial; or it is the denial of this pseudo-essence as an objective being dwelling outside man and independent of him, and its transformation into the subject" (p. 159).

A more concrete contextualization or interpretation of Hegel's negation of the negation takes place when Marx describes the process as "the *appropriation* of the objective essence through the annulment of its estrangement" (p. 161). An example here is the annulment of God and private property as "the advent of theoretic humanism" (i.e., atheism) and "the justification of real human life as man's possession and thus the advent of practical humanism" (i.e., communism) (p. 161). Drawing a clear distinction between communism and atheism and Hegel's end point, Absolute Knowledge, Marx states that these entail "no abstraction...[and no] primitive simplicity...On the contrary, they are but the first real coming-to-be, the realization become real for man, of man's essence—of the essence of man as something real" (p. 161). Making this point in *Marx and Education*, Robin Small (2005) notes that while Marx agreed with Feuerbach that religion works to alienate humanity from itself by permanently displacing itself in an abstract God, atheism is limited by the fact that it is a theoretical position:

> Atheism...overcomes alienation with the realm of thought, but it does not overcome the alienation of thought itself—that is, the alienation of thought from the other aspects of human life. Atheism remains a theoretical standpoint, with all the drawbacks that this implies: abstractness, unreality and irrelevance to the practical concerns of humanity. Still needed is the reunification of the theoretical and the practical which only revolutionary activity can accomplish. (p. 26)

The message here, however, is not to conveniently replace atheism with communism, as many religious Marxists have done. The point is rather that the critique of ideology or discourse—religious or otherwise—is severely limited without a concrete mass movement aimed at transforming the real, objective conditions of people's lives and the very relations of production that underlie the material basis of (bourgeois) society.

This is a central starting point of a critical pedagogy of becoming: to use education as a vehicle through which students and teachers can begin self-reflecting on our internalized "reason as unreason" that comprises the central epistemology of the dominant ideology. Critical pedagogy, at its best, challenges students to become conscious of their own consciousness as part of the process of self-transformation. For example, coming to know one's position within capitalism as a wealth-generating commodity, and thus as alienated existence, can lead to self-consciousness. But again, Marx pushes us beyond the estrangement of thought alone and forces us to consider the concrete objectivity of the source of estrangement situated in the context of the social nature of human existence (i.e., contrary to the romantic mythology of bour-geois ideology, the development of productive forces is always and unavoid-ably social)—in this case capitalism itself—and thus the need for a concrete, collective, social movement to transcend the labor-capital relation that pre-vents the development of the productive forces in a direction toward general *coming-to-be*.

Peter McLaren has taken a version of this Marxist Humanism as a cen-tral influence in his own approach to critical pedagogy. Paramount to this approach is Marx's interpretation or correction of Hegel's concept of the ne-gation of the negation, which, again, implies the complete negation or tran-scendence of a real, concrete social system, such as feudalism or capitalism, and the simultaneous emergence and movement toward a new basis of human sociability (i.e., communism). Breaking from utopian socialism, Marx was specifically interested in *how, when, why,* and by *whom* the *what is* can devel-op into the *what can be*. Following Hudis here, McLaren also draws on the work of Raya Dunayevskaya, a Marxist theoretician, philosopher, and revolu-tionary who further developed Marx's Hegelian dialectics in the 1950s after breaking from Stalinism and then Trotskyism (Hudis & Anderson, 2002). In collaboration with the Trinidadian revolutionary, C.L.R. James and others Dunayevskaya continued the development of Marx's humanism. In the 1950s, Dunayevskaya, frustrated with what she felt was the vulgar simplicity of Soviet Communism, justifying state-sanctioned exploitation and violence, revisited the relationship between Hegel and Marx. In the process, she read Hegel, as Marx did, for the revolutionary potential within the negation of the nega-tion. Summarizing what they argue was Dunayevskaya's major contribution to Hegelian Marxism, Hudis and Anderson (2002) note that it:

> ...centers on what many other Marxists have ignored or rejected—Hegel's concept of *absolute* negativity. In Hegel, absolute negativity signifies not only the negation of external obstacles, but also the negation of the earlier negation. The power of nega-tivity gets turned back upon the self, upon the internal as well as external barriers to self-movement. Such a negation of the negation is no mere nullity, for the positive is contained in the negative, which is the path to a new beginning. (p. xviii)

Hegel's concept of the force that generates the movement that Hudis and Anderson refer to here is contradiction. It is contradiction that gives purpose and motivation to the concept of critical pedagogy. One of the main con-tradictions to which critical pedagogy attends is that between the promise of bourgeois ideology—that capitalism is the system that guarantees freedom and equality (and thus *becoming*)—and the reality of bourgeois society—that it only ever delivers general poverty, exploitation, oppression, and alienation. Again, the contradiction referred to by Hegel is contradictory existence, which Marx re-contextualizes within the sensuousness of the suffering human.

The wageworker in general, living in and out of various degrees of exploitation and alienation, embodies his or her own negation as such, and thus the potential to become his or her own Other, already embodied within the laboring classes. This is a reconceptualization of Hegel's positive contained within the negative. However, this potential positive within absolute negativity is not a guaranteed or predetermined product of the negation of the negation. The end of capitalism does not guarantee communism. Critical pedagogy is therefore a call to action to take a militant stance and play a purposive role in pushing against the negative potential toward communism. For example, summarizing Freire's revolutionary, solidarity-based approach to class struggle, Antonia Darder (2009) comments:

> …Freire's work was unabashedly grounded in Marxist-Socialist thought…[F]or Freire, the struggle against economic domination could not be waged effectively without a humanizing praxis that could both engage the complex phenomena of class struggle and effectively foster the conditions for critical social agency among the masses…Although he openly acknowledged the existence of racism, he was reticent to abandon the notion of class struggle…He insisted that the struggle against oppression was a human struggle in which we had to build solidarity across our differences, if we were to change a world engulfed by capitalism. (pp. 570–571)

Darder's insights here could not be more important situated in the context of a larger critical pedagogy community that has disconnected a Marxist class analysis from the focus on race, gender, and identity. Making her point absolutely clear, Darder (2009) emphasizes that the purpose of critical pedagogy is to subvert domination and that without an adequate theory of the historical development of capitalism and all its contradictions and determinations, a well-thought-out critical pedagogy pointing to the *positive* within the *negative* is an unlikely outcome. Offering a similar example of a Freirean approach to critical pedagogy, Henry Giroux (2013) notes that such a pedagogy, "unlike dominant modes of teaching, insists that one of the fundamental tasks of educators is to make sure that the future points the way to a more socially just world" (p. xiv). McLaren (2005) articulates this purpose of critical pedagogy, yet, like Darder, more concretely situated within the Marxist Humanist tradition and without the vague references to "social justice":

The ideological formations intergenerationally reproduced within schools betray a pragmatic efficacy and validity of apologetic purpose as well as the fetishistic character of everyday thinking. Such formations help to orient students into an unreflexive acceptance of the capitalistic world. Of course, the accession into the social order has always been incomplete, always in process, in that there has always been a space between self-formation and its dismemberment. Critical pedagogy seizes upon this space as its major terrain of struggle. (p. 23)

That is, the existence of internal contradictions, which exist within all entities, represents the force that compels but does not determine human societies to change and develop. Callinicos (2011), another contemporary Marxist scholar and activist that McLaren has engaged, describes this tendency toward perpetual change and growth using the example of the acorn and the oak tree. Consider:

The acorn, in becoming an oak, has itself ceased to be. The oak is different from the acorn. The oak is *not* that acorn. Hegel would say that the oak is the *negation* of the acorn. Yet implicit within the acorn is the potential to become an oak. The acorn contains within itself its own negation, and is thus *contradictory*. It is this contradiction…that allows it to grow…Hegel then takes this a step further. When something negates itself it turns into its opposite. (p. 63)

Callinicos here offers a way to conceptualize change from a sort of Hegelian-Marxist point of view, although such botanical explanations of change and development are far too passive for Marx's dialectical materialist approach. Growth or development, what has been called movement, is a never-ending process. This conception of the human condition can be seen functioning at the center of Freire's work (Blunden, 2013), which is the starting point for critical pedagogy in general. Using the framework outlined by Callinicos, we can replace "acorn" with *alienated worker* and "oak tree" with *non-alienated humanity freely engaged in a planned, collective effort to reproduce social existence.* The Marxist dialectic allows us to understand that the potential to be free—to reunite thinking and doing—already exists within the alienated wageworker, from the privileged engineers and managers to the more oppressed manual laborers. Those of us who rely on a wage to survive are therefore contradictory—we embody our own potential negation as dehumanized existence because our vital powers, our humanness, are externally commanded and controlled.

The basis for a new society, in other words, already exists within us as a potential. But if a new society is to be the negation of what exists, what might Marx's developing conception of the opposite of capital offer our understanding here? As we will see below, Marx's work retained its Hegelian roots over time, even as he changed and refined it, discarding much of the Hegelian rhetoric along the way. In Marx's *Grundrisse*, the notebooks, with arguably the heaviest Hegelian language since his *1844 Manuscripts*, Marx (1939/1973) elaborates on capital's opposite, one of the central contradictions or antagonisms at the heart of capital:

> The opposite of capital cannot itself be a particular commodity, for as such it would form no opposition to capital, since the substance of capital is itself use value; it is not this commodity or that commodity, but all commodities. The communal substance of all commodities, i.e. their substance not as material stuff, as physical character, but their communal substance as commodities and hence exchange values, is this, that they are objectified labour. The only thing distinct from objectified labour is non-objectified labour, labour which is still objectifying itself, labour as subjectivity. Or, objectified labour, i.e. labour which is present in space, can also be opposed, as past labour, to labour which is present in time. If it is to be present in time, alive, then it can be present only as the living subject, in which it exists as capacity, as possibility; hence as worker. The only use value, therefore, which can form the opposite pole to capital is labour. (p. 207)

Marx's conceptualization of the commodity is reflective of Hegel's chapters on absolutes in *Logic*. The opposite of the living laborer, of labor potential, for Marx, is dead labor, or expended labor congealed into a commodity. The opposite of capital, the laborer, as future profit, profit that enriches and thus empowers the capitalist to dominate the laborer, is contradictory and embodies his or her own negation as alienated and exploited labor-power. The opposite of labor as alienated subjectivity is therefore non-alienated humanity engaged in free associations with each other, planning and reproducing their existence as the product of the unification of thinking and doing. In this context, each person is a producer, and each producer has a vested interest in participating in the decisions concerning what, how, and with whom they produce because each one has no method of surviving in this world but through the products of their labor and the necessary interrelationships that this production entails. Here work is not an external, alienated means of meeting one's immediate needs but rather satisfies basic social needs themselves. Humanization is thus the production of a political, economic, and social world that facilitates the material requirements for being and becoming, and it is to this humanization that Marxist critical pedagogy refers. Making a similar point, McLaren (2005) identifies what he sees as critical pedagogy's most central internal challenge as it presses forward:

The struggle among what Marx called our "vital powers," our dispositions, our inner selves and our objective outside, our human capacities and competencies and the social formations within which they are produced, *ensures* the production of a form of human agency that reflects the contradictions within capitalist social life…Critical educators must play a role in preventing the domestication of the general intellect, and directly challenge capital in its role in reifying and commodifying the production of emancipatory knowledge, of a critical social brain. (pp. 56–57)

It is this critical pedagogy driven by a deep desire to know and to transcend that pushes the critical educator to search out new tools that students and teachers can use to deepen our perspectives and critical thinking skills. One way in which to do this is to consider the complexity and diversity of the current capitalist system and the way in which it is characterized by a continuum of alienation where some forms of livelihood are more alienating than others. This continuum offers a glimpse into the potential of a non-alienated existence, which is always a difficult task for students—that is, imagining a life after capital (McLaren, 2005). For example, U.S. capitalist society is large enough to support many independent craftsmen who do not sell their labor capacity to a capitalist to generate more wealth but to individuals as a form of consuming revenue. Discussing this phenomenon, Marx (1939/1973) elaborates:

Labour as mere performance of services for the satisfaction of immediate needs has nothing whatever to do with capital, since that is not capital's concern. If a capitalist hires a woodcutter to chop wood to roast his mutton over, then not only does the wood-cutter relate to the capitalist, but also the capitalist to the woodcutter, in the relation of simple exchange. The woodcutter gives him his service, a use value, which does not increase capital; rather, capital consumes itself in it; and the capitalist gives him another commodity for it in the form of money. The same relation holds for all services which workers exchange directly for the money of other persons, and which are consumed by these persons. This is consumption of revenue, which, as such, always falls within simple circulation; it is not consumption of capital. Since one of the contracting parties does not confront the other as a capitalist, this performance of a service cannot fall under the category of productive labour. (p. 208)

While Marx was drawing this example to underscore what specifically is required for labor to be productive in the capitalist sense, we can see a less alienated and less coerced existence within the life of Marx's independent woodcutter or carpenter than in the factory worker or the teacher working at a for-profit privatized charter school expected to follow a scripted curriculum and whose job security rests on her students' annual standardized test scores. Following this movement, a Marxist critical pedagogy challenges us to not only understand the historical process that led to capitalism and its real subjection of all forms of labor, but it challenges us to imagine ourselves in a world where the labor-capital relationship had been negated completely/absolutely. While we must not nurture the illusion of a backwards movement to pre-capitalist social relations, one way in which this can be done is by seeking out alternative forms of production within the present.

Critical Pedagogy and the Falling Rate of Profit

Again, collectively, laborers across the planet embody the knowledge and ability of the current global society that is more than capable of meeting everyone's material needs. The world as it exists is both the source of today's dehumanized existence as well as the source of humanization—it is both the problem and the solution; it is contradictory, and thus compelled but not predetermined to change. The negation of ourselves as alienated objects is therefore as present within ourselves as it is within the acorn to negate itself in the process of becoming an oak tree. What is it, then, that prevents humanity from engaging in the process of *becoming*? This all-important question is the driving force behind this book, and there certainly are many answers to this question, and these answers change in accordance with the particular state and strategies of capital at any given time. Yet there is no doubt that one of the threads that connects these various answers has to do with the ideological conception of ourselves as individuals who are disconnected from larger social forces. Another way of phrasing this is to say that the process of becoming communist is straightjacketed by the way in which we think of—and live—the relationship between the objective and the subjective. What we want to do in the rest of this chapter is to turn to Marx's analysis of the falling rate of profit to articulate a more appropriate way of understanding and living this relationship.

Following the Civil War, the U.S. saw a surge in industrial output coupled with a spike in college enrollments, from 1,000 to 65,000. Similarly, in the years immediately following WWII, college enrollments increased from 1 million to 11 million (Malott, 2014). How do we make sense of these surges in educational attainment—surges that offered many working-class people, especially the white working class, a degree of upward mobility? Do these spikes in college-educated workers represent the bourgeois promise of general equality and the flourishing of democratic ideals? Or do these changes reflect the changing needs of capital as the demand for U.S. manufactured goods exploded on a national and then global basis?

If we are to view capitalist schooling as serving the needs of capital by educating the kind of workers required by capital, then these surges in education point to the perpetually declining proportion of capital being invested in variable capital (human labor power) and the simultaneous increase of investments in constant capital, that is, in labor-saving technology as capitalists compete for market share and competitive advantage driving down, over time, the rate of profit. This is the primary force that has lead to the cyclical nature of crisis in capitalism. In short, we might call this the recurring *historical event* relevant to the development of capitalism—the cycle of deepening crisis fuelled by the tendency toward the falling rate of profit—a major contradiction one would think would lead to widespread working-class consciousness, critical agency, and, ultimately, change (i.e., the negation of the negation). After many years of theoretical development, in the third volume of *Capital*, Marx (1894/1981) describes the falling rate of profit in the following terms:

> The relative decline in the variable capital and increase in the constant capital, even while both grow in absolute terms, is…simply another expression for the increased productivity of labor…[W]ith the progress of capitalist production, the mass of value that must simply be reproduced and maintained rises and grows with the rising productivity of labor, even if the labor-power applied remains constant. (pp. 322–324)

While Marx is describing what he identifies as one of the fundamental laws of capitalist production, he took the concept from classical political economic theory and developed it through many notebooks and over the course of many years. Making this point in "Crisis and the Rate of Profit in Marx's Laboratory," Peter Thomas and Geert Reuten (2013) argue that "Marx's views on the 'law' or 'tendency' of the rate of profit to fall developed throughout his life from a law about the historical destination of the capitalist system as tending toward breakdown, into a theory about the functioning of the capitalist mode of production as a potentially durable system" (p. 312). Marx's humanist or naturalist framework developed in his 1844 manuscripts allowed him the freedom to develop his ideas based upon reflections on the real, concrete world, unlike Hegel's work, which is hopelessly tethered to the abstractness of the *essence* of the *absolute idea*.

In his earlier dealings with the subject, such as his 1857–1858 *Grundrisse* notebooks, he focused on the internal laws of the historical development of capital as the contradiction or force that would self-destructively lead to the violent overthrow of capitalism—the negation of the negation, as it were. As an example of what they refer to as Marx's "crisis rhetoric," Thomas and Reuten (2013) cite the *Grundrisse*:

> The growing incompatibility between the productive development of society and its hitherto existing relations of production expresses itself in bitter contradictions, crises, spasms. The violent destruction of capital not by relations external to it, but rather as a condition of its self-preservation... These contradictions lead to explosions, cataclysms, crises, in which momentous suspension of labor and annihilation of a great portion of capital the latter is violently reduced to the point where it can go on...Yet, these regularly recurring catastrophes lead to their repetition on a higher scale, and finally to its violent overthrow. (p. 314)

Thomas and Reuten (2013) argue that at this time, Marx was still under the influence of the young Hegelians, who deterministically saw the economic crisis of 1848 as the precursor to the end of capitalism—an end that was not the result of an organized critically conscious, working-class agency but the inevitable conclusion of the development of the internal contradictions of an economic system operating by its own laws independent of human intervention (i.e., like the passive negation of the acorn driven by an internal genetic code). In other words, Hegel's dialectic, the negation of the negation, was viewed as unfolding deterministically without, or despite, human intervention. Years after the predictions of the economic determinists failed to pass, Marx began rethinking the destructive role of the tendency for the rate of profit to fall as less *terminal* and more *restorative*.

Citing the 1861–3 notebooks as indicative of this shift in Marx's thinking, Thomas and Reuten (2013) quote, "...apart from theory there is also the practice, the crises from superabundance of capital, or, what comes to the same, the mad ventures capital enters upon in consequence of the lowering of the rate of profit. Hence crises...acknowledged as a necessary violent means for the cure of the plethora of capital, and the restoration of a sound rate of profit" (p. 319). Marx began to see the crises stemming from the contradictory tendency toward the fall in the rate of profit as allowing the process of capitalist accumulation to begin anew and therefore an integral component of developing *the productive power of capital*. No longer did Marx express crises and the falling rate of profit as "the gravedigger of the capitalist mode of production" (Thomas & Reuten, 2013, p. 319). Thwarting the deterministic unfolding of capital's internal contradictions, it would seem, is the role of human agency. Capital's interest resides within moving human agency toward supporting capital, toward maintaining the hegemony. The role of a Marxist-informed critical pedagogy, on the other hand, is committed to counter hegemony (McLaren, 2005).

In stressing the *tendential* nature of the falling rate of profit, Marx not only elaborated on the productive role of destruction or crises driven by the internal logic of capital, but he explored the measures capitalists themselves— expressed as human beings with choice and agency—take to counter the falling rate of profit. "Explaining why this fall is not greater or faster," Marx (1894/1981) notes that "counteracting influences must be at work, checking and cancelling the effect of the general law and giving it simply the character of a tendency, which is why we have described the fall in the general rate of profit as a tendential fall" (p. 339). Summarizing these "counteracting influences," David Harvey (2014), in a recent book on capital's contradictions, describes them as "labor saving innovations," which, in the contemporary context, include:

> The opening up of entirely new product lines that were labor-intensive; a pattern of innovation that was devoted as much to capital saving as to labor saving; a rising rate of exploitation on the labor-forces still employed; the prior existence or formation of a class of consumers who produced nothing; a phenomenal rate of growth in the total labor force which would augment the mass of capital being produced even though the individual rate of return was falling. (p. 107)

However, while counteracting forces such as increasing the rate of exploitation of labor help to explain the general laws' tendential manifestation, they are, ironically, also the same factors that speed it up. Marx (1894/1981) comments that "these factors that inhibit the fall in the rate of profit... in the final instance they always accelerate it further" (pp. 340–341). Extending his comments here, Marx argues that the falling rate of profit operates:

> [A]s a law whose absolute realization is held up, delayed and weakened by counter-acting factors. However, as the same factors that increase the rate of surplus-value (and the extension of the working day is itself a result of large-scale industry) tend to reduce the amount of labor-power employed by a given capital, the same factors tend both to reduce the rate of profit and to slow down the movement in this direction. (pp. 341–342)

Again, Marx is getting at one of the central contradictions or paradoxes of capital here: as the mass of labor-power set in motion by capital increases, and with it, accumulated value or profit, the rate of profit actually decreases. This tendency leads to stagnation and crisis. Again, rather than immediately and inevitably leading to the violent overthrow of capitalism, Marx began to see crises operating in a different way. Counteracting forces—such as increasing the rate of exploitation and relying heavily on consumer debt for value realization—while leading to crisis and the breakdown in the business cycle, serve as a kind of contemporary primitive accumulation enriching and revitalizing today's most powerful capitalists, the bankers and financiers.

Similarly, Mészáros (2011) calls capital's attempts to prevent its own self-destruction a form of *hybridization* where the state intervenes on behalf of corporations. However, looking at the concrete context and conditions of capital since the 1970s, Mészáros does not see crisis and capital's attempts to displace it as restorative. While some restorative measures can be identified at work, such as the Great Depression and the World Wars, current measures (i.e., militarism, neoliberalism, etc.) are simply unable to overcome the crisis. Mészáros takes his cues from Marx and looks to the social structure of capital and the determinations it embodies as providing a framework for the system's historical development. For example, capital is a system based upon perpetual growth and economic expansion, but planet Earth is not decidedly infinite, and currently, there are no significant regions where capital has not expanded. Without an ability to expand, capital faces serious structural problems that are simply not resolvable. Clearly, Mészáros (2011), while acknowledging the needed working-class agency to transcend capital before it destroys all that exists, focuses on hidden mechanisms or the internal logic of capital.

While these contradictions are not resolvable within capitalism, they are displaceable and moveable. Thus, while capital can no longer expand *absolutely*, it can expand *relatively* by reshaping the globe again and again. Examining the spatial manifestations of these contradictions led Neil Smith (1984/2008) to develop the "seesaw theory" of uneven development:

> Capital moves to where the rate of profit is highest (or at least high), and these moves are synchronized with the rhythm of accumulation and crisis. The mobility of capital brings about the development of areas with a high rate of profit and the underdevelopment of those areas where a low rate of profit pertains. But the process of development itself leads to the diminution of this higher rate of profit. (p. 197)

In other words, investment of capital in one area (city, region, nation) of the globe is accompanied by disinvestment in another. Yet as the returns on investment in the former area diminish, capital flows back to a formerly disinvested area.

Challenging this focus on the *laws* of capital in the late 1970s, Antonio Negri published a widely influential book, *Marx Beyond Marx: Lessons on the Grundrisse*. Negri (1991) takes issue with Marx's "objectivist" conception of the historical development of capital that is grounded in an analysis of *structural determinations*. For example, in his discussion of the falling rate of profit, Marx identifies the force that propels it as embedded within the very structure of capital itself. For Negri, it is not the laws of capitalist production but the subjectivity of labor that the capitalist class is forced to respond to that drives the historical development of capitalism. In his critically important and controversial text, *Marx's Concept of the Alternative to Capitalism*, Peter Hudis (2012) argues that while "Negri's effort to account for agency illuminates important aspects of Marx's work," his exaggerated analysis assumes that "every stage of capitalist development is a product of heightened subjective resistance" (p. 30). The neoliberal era of capitalism, for Negri (1991), is not the result of the internal logic of capital mediated by human actors but is a result of new forms of discipline developed by capital as a response to "intensifying subjective resistance" (Hudis, 2012, p. 30). In the Introduction to the 1991 Autonomedia edition of *Marx Beyond Marx*, Harry Cleaver (1991) offers a powerful summary of the significance of the subjective resistance of labor at the heart of Negri's work:

> Marx is keenly aware that capital's power to extort surplus labor is a power exerted over an "other" whose own active subjectivity must be harnessed to capital's designs. Marx explored this subjectivity and saw that it fought the primitive accumulation of the classes: the forced creation of the labor market and the forced submission of people to the lives of workers. He explored this subjectivity and saw that *it struggles against being forced to work*. Although he paints a true horror story of living labor being dominated by capitalist-controlled dead labor, Marx also makes clear that living labor cannot be killed off totally or capital itself would die. The irony of capitalist reproduction is that it must assure the continued reproduction of the living subject. The antagonism is recreated on higher and higher levels as capital develops. What begins as the horror of zombie-like dead labor being summoned against living labor, becomes, over time, an increasingly desperate attempt by capital to protect its own existence against an ever-more-powerful-and-hostile working class. Capital can never win, totally, once and for ever. It must tolerate the existence of an alien subjectivity which constantly threatens to destroy it. What a vision: capital, living in everlasting fear of losing control over the hostile class it has brought into existence! (p. xxiii)

What is apparent here is Cleaver's ability to demonstrate, via Marx, the inherent conflict between the contradictory class interests that have, no doubt, influenced the historical development of capital. However, what Cleaver

(1991) and Negri (1991) pay less attention to are the socializing and thus hegemonizing influences of not only education and the dominant culture of bourgeois society but the act of work itself, where selling oneself on the market for a wage becomes so commonplace and taken-for-granted that it rarely is the subject of critique or discussion, let alone a working-class movement against it.

While we agree that Negri helps illuminate the importance of working-class subjectivity, in this book, we want to locate—as Negri fails to do— this subjectivity as produced within the internal laws and logic of capital. In other words, both subjectivist and objectivist orientations are important for understanding the totality of the social universe of capital. The internal contradictions of capital compel it toward absolute negation, but the agency of humans facing each other antagonistically pushes and pulls toward and away from transcendence. Put another way, we are advocating taking a more objectivist approach focusing on the internal logic of capital and the subsequent tendency toward the falling rate of profit needed to develop a complex understanding of subjective resistance and a subsequent, purposeful, critical pedagogy—a pedagogy of *becoming*.

The Falling Rate of Profit and the Indebted Student

From an objectivist perspective, the current era of capital represents in part the capitalist response to counter the falling rate of profit beginning in the early 1970s. We might note that WWII enabled the U.S. to emerge from the economic crisis of the 1929 Stock Market crash and decade-long Great Depression as an unprecedented super power. One of the most significant factors contributing to global U.S. economic and militaristic hegemony was the fact that the industrial infrastructures of China, Germany, France, England, and Japan had been obliterated by the destruction of war. Consequently, after WWII, U.S. manufacturers were in an unprecedented state of global advantage with their international competitors virtually bombed out of existence (Malott, 2014).

Consequently, U.S. industrial capitalists' need for more managers, engineers, professors, etc. boomed. That is, the supply of highly educated workers, as was the case during the industrial surge following the Civil War, was below capital's demand. It is for this reason that immediately following WWII, public higher education enrollment increased from 2 million to 11 million, giving working people in the U.S. the sense that general prosperity was achievable within capitalism as bourgeois revolutionaries had always asserted. However, around the 1970s, the U.S. post-WWII boom began to decline, as international competition had recovered from the devastation of war and capitalists worldwide began to push back against the growing power of labor. The capitalist state's support for public higher education has been declining ever since. Today, the supply of highly educated workers is far greater than capital's demand due to a host of factors including technological developments and the shifting of centers of production to developing nations and the so-called third world made possible by free-trade agreements, robotics, and computerization (Malott, 2014).

Put another way, this international competition led to a technological race in computerization and robotics that resulted in improvements in production efficiency and the creation of many new markets (especially in electronics). This competitive race at the heart of the internal logic of capital, over time, requires a growing proportion of investments going to machines and technology rather than to the purchasing of productive labor-power capacity, leading to a falling rate of profit and crisis. In other words, as production becomes more efficient, it becomes more costly, eating up more potential profits in the production process. This is the result of another key contradiction in capital: the contradiction between the individual capitalist and the capitalist class as a whole. It is in the interest of each individual capitalist to develop and employ labor-saving machinery, as this enables them to capture a greater portion of relative surplus-value. Yet, as this machinery becomes generalized, this process decreases the absolute mass of surplus-value, which runs completely counter to the interests of the capitalist class.

Again, the economic crisis of the 1970s can be understood as stemming, in part, from international competition and the subsequent falling rate of profit. Situating this current crisis in a global context, Harvey (2014) notes:

> Developmental paths of this sort have effectively held off falling profits for some time now. The absorption of the peasantries of China, India and much of South-East Asia (along with Turkey and Egypt and some Latin American countries, with Africa still the continent with massive untapped labor reserves) into the global labor force since 1980 or so, along with the integration of what was the Soviet Bloc, has meant a huge increase (rather than decrease) in the global wage labor force over and beyond that supplied by population growth. The rising rates of exploitation with the creation of horrific labor conditions in China, Bangladesh, Vietnam and elsewhere are also palpable, while the demand problem has largely been taken care of by way of a vast expansion of credit. (pp. 107–108)

Neoliberal policies and ideology can be understood as a contemporary shift to counter the falling rate of profit, operating in this dual way, leading to an unprecedented concentration of wealth at the top while simultaneously slowing accumulation down. With 80% of Americans, for example, at or near the poverty line, the notion of general prosperity within capitalism reveals itself as bitter mockery. This insight can be understood, in part, by underscoring the very relationship between labor and capital itself.

While forms of wage labor existed during feudalism, segments of the peasant population enjoyed too many entitlements to life's most vital use-values, presenting a barrier to "the possibility of capitalistic wealth" (Marx, 1939/1973, p. 274). In other words, as we will see below, a fundamental requirement or condition for capitalist production relations to solidify is an ever-expanding pool of dependent wage laborers who have no other option to survive but to exchange their own labor for exchange-value, for an equivalent (i.e., money) that can be exchanged for any other product of labor.

In the exchange between labor and capital, which labor is compelled to engage in, labor sells her commodity (i.e., labor-power) to the capitalist for a price, needed to access other use-values. The use-value the capitalist obtains is labor-power, "the productive force which maintains and multiplies capital, and which thereby becomes the productive force, the reproductive force of capital, a force belonging to capital itself" (p. 274). In the historical development of capitalism, we find absolutely no examples of widespread voluntary expropriation and thus self-imposed dependence. As capitalism develops through time, the productivity of labor is increased through labor-saving technology and more effective educational and training pedagogies, represented in a greater portion of capitalist investment being consumed by constant capital, leading to the falling rate of profit.

Neoliberal tactics to counter the falling rate of profit include, but are not limited to: the elimination of competition through monopolization; increasing the rate of exploitation; U.S. military intervention nearly eliminating the cost of labor in the so-called third world for foreign investors; "free trade" policies that really amount to a form of protectionism designed to limit international competition; and one of the most significant mechanisms, as it relates to education, has been financialization, represented by a dramatic shift in investment from productive capital to money capital. Ideologically, this has been accompanied by abandoning commitments to the welfare state and the public in general as socialist, un-American, or an attack on freedom.

Financialization creates the appearance of growth, which may have no material basis. Rising profits in the financial sector do not necessarily come from real growth but the plundering of public resources. In their quest for new markets and new sources of profit in an increasingly technicized world, the public sector has been a major target for hungry investors desperate to set capitals in motion to engage the process of expansion and accumulation. One strategy plays out something like this: taxes are reduced on the capitalist class; education is cut as state coffers dry up; the quality of said programs becomes degraded; the public is thus more easily convinced that the problem with education, ironically, is that it lacks competition; privatization is proffered as the only solution.

One profound way in which this transfer has taken place has been through the normalization and generalization of business language, which now dominates education. Education is now conceived of as an economic transaction, positioning the learner as a (indebted) consumer with a demand for knowledge and the teacher and educational institution or site (public, private, or hybrid) as the supplier of that knowledge. Biesta (2006) summarizes its effects as follows:

> ... to think of education as an economic transaction only misconstrues the role of the learner and the educator in the educational relationship, it also results in a situation in which questions about the content and purpose of education become subject to the forces of the market instead of being the concern of professional judgment and democratic deliberation. (p. 31)

Students in this context are not respected for their unique positionalities and potential or actual critical agency but are disrespected as mere customers or economic entities and thus sources of profit. Again, much of this profit is not the result of real economic growth but the result of growing student debt, and debt can only displace crisis for so long. Teachers and professors must not be thought of as potential political militants or—particularly under neoliberalism—even stewards of the common good, but mechanistic product deliverers. It is therefore increasingly difficult to enact critical pedagogy in this savage context.

Systems of public higher education, consequently, once a necessary cost of the reproduction of labor-power, are now treated as sources of profit as tuitions skyrocket and students are saddled with crushing debt in a world with fewer and fewer employment opportunities. Contributing to our understanding here,

Marx (1867/1983) offers a concise explanation of the role of debt in capitalist economics:

> The public debt becomes one of the most powerful levers of primitive accumulation. As with the stroke of an enchanter's wand, it endows barren money with the power of breeding and thus turns it into capital, without the necessity of its exposing itself to the troubles and risks inseparable from its employment in industry or even in usury... The national debt has given rise to...stock-exchange and gambling and the modern bankocracy... [Debt is] the best system for making the wage-laborer submissive, frugal, industrious, and overburdened with labor. (pp. 754–756)

Because of falling wages (accompanied by longer work hours) in the so-called first world since the 1970s, debt has been used to keep consumption apace with global production and to discipline an increasingly alienated and impoverished work force. Privatized systems of education have produced fortunes off of student debt. Meanwhile, the elite institutions, the Harvards, will remain unscathed, as working-class universities are sacrificed to appease the angry gods of the market. The financialization or privatization of charter schools and universities is contributing to the erosion of unionization, which is at a 100-year low at 11.3% of the total workforce, contributing to the redistribution of wealth upwards and escalating immiseration, again, countering the falling rate of profit without increasing real productive output. As of now, there exists no real plan or vision for widespread prosperity coming from either faction of the capitalist class. University presidents at public institutions, for example, increasingly refer to this as the new normal—a downward spiral of perpetual budget cuts suggesting privatization is inevitable and somehow good. Democracy has been redefined as profit making and cutthroat competition between workers (Giroux, 2013).

While all workers have taken substantial economic blows in the neoliberal era, Black and Latino people are increasingly offered to whites as scapegoats for economic crisis. This has had deadly consequences, which we explore in Chapter 5. As Giroux has recently pointed out, the welfare state has been replaced by the punishing state, the surveillance state, the incarcerating state targeting Blacks and Latinos at alarming rates. This is the larger context of neoliberalism. That is, in the U.S., neoliberal economic policy has effectively countered the falling rate of profit at the expense of the working people of the world. Neoliberal economic policy would not have been successful without a strong ideological component. Hegemony, in other words, works to prevent the growing contradictions of capital from leading to the type of paradigmatic change that facilitates becoming.

Conclusion

In this opening chapter, we have sought to examine precisely what the process of *becoming* is in critical pedagogy. While critical pedagogy has been the victim of a general liberalization that has severed its radical potential, even some iterations of radical critical pedagogy have been limited to a critique of the present. We wish to critique and understand the present but always with the intention of negation. Thus, central to this critical pedagogy of becoming is the dialectical movement of negation. In order to understand this, we have surveyed Marx's take on—and transformation of—Hegelian dialectics. Through this process, we demonstrated that Marx did not radically break from Hegel but rather immanently transformed Hegelian dialectics through radical critique and challenge. Just as Marx brought dialectics back to earth, situating the dialectical movement within the production of the system of nature, so too have we insisted that the process of becoming communist is not only an ideological struggle but a struggle over the structural determinants of life—that web of materiality through which ourselves and our social relations are made possible.

· 2 ·

FROM REVOLUTION TO COUNTERREVOLUTION AND BACK AGAIN? THE GLOBAL CLASS WAR AND BECOMING COMMUNIST

Introduction

Critical pedagogy is an intervention in the present order of things, a force of contestation that not only insists that there *are* alternatives to present social formations but, more importantly, also develops a vision of what those alternatives might look like, or at least some elements of what they entail. And, as we will continue to stress, the process of becoming other cannot but begin with the present. As such, critical pedagogy must have an adequate understanding of the current moment, of the determinations of our time. Such an understanding of the determinations of our time first demands that we grasp the historical forces that have placed us here, those "circumstances directly encountered, given and transmitted from the past" (Marx, 1852/1972, p. 15). This chapter works to construct a narrative of the determinants of contemporary critical pedagogy, asserting the *primacy of the international situation*.

While there is no shortage of talk about neoliberalism today—in critical education and elsewhere—we here define our contemporary moment as one that is dominated by *counterrevolution*. Such an appraisal might at first seem dramatic or even pessimistic; for there are, to be sure, promising sparks of uprisings routinely occurring, flickers of protest and social movements, and sustained flames of resistance across the globe. In some parts of the world, resistance movements even hold political, military, social, and economic power. But compared to the circuit of socialist and national liberation struggles that swept the world during the 20th century, providing an effective counterweight to imperialism and a pole around which the world's workers and oppressed could congregate, the period from roughly 1979 until today has been one of reaction against such struggles. The gains made by oppressed peoples, beginning with the 1917 Bolshevik Revolution, have been the focal point of a concerted attack by international capitalists and imperialists. We argue that the present contours of the class struggle are best grasped through a historical examination of the *global class war*, a framework developed by Sam Marcy in the 1950s. This framework is more expansive and accurate than "neoliberalism," although we demonstrate below that neoliberalism is part of a broader global capitalist class strategy.

In this chapter, we draw on the first volume of *Capital*, offering key insights into how the characteristics of the contemporary neoliberal era represent a continuation of the logic of capital, which, in the larger context, is the global class war. In this chapter, we focus again on the working-class agency pushing against the terrorist energy inherent to the internal drive and spirit of capital. In the first part of the chapter, we explore the concept of neoliberalism and situate it within the historical development of capital itself by exploring concepts related to Marx's discussion of primitive accumulation. From here, we transition into our deeper discussion of the global class war between the imperialist and proletarian camps. We examine the 20th century through this lens, arguing that this—and not neoliberalism—provides a more comprehensive framework for understanding the contemporary waters of revolutionary pedagogy and socialist movements. We pay special attention to China, offering a more nuanced and class-conscious conception of China's Communist Party and the socialist potential it continues to possess. At the end, we offer some concluding comments on how the present text contributes to our project of building a Marxist critical pedagogy of becoming for a communist future.

Neoliberalism: A Necessary but Incomplete Framework

There seems to be a growing consensus that we are living in an age defined as "neoliberal." It is not only critical pedagogues who have mobilized this term but all sorts of critical, progressive, and even liberal educators. At the 2014 meeting of the American Educational Studies Association, for example, there were 31 presentations with the word "neoliberal" in the title. Yet preventing any such consensus are two problems. The first problem is that neoliberalism is a fairly chaotic and nebulous signifier, one that can have as many definitions as there are journal articles concerned with the term. The second problem is that neoliberalism can also be an empty signifier, one that is not even defined. In a recent study, Julie Rowlands and Shaun Rawolle (2013) collected data on how the word "neoliberalism" and its variants, such as neo-liberal, have been utilized in peer-reviewed English-language education journal articles that contained the word "neoliberalism" in their titles. The purpose of the study was to determine how and, really, *if*, the term is being conceptualized within educational research. What they found was that, out of 110 articles studied, 29 gave substantive definitions of neoliberalism (at least two paragraphs), 27 gave brief definitions (up to one paragraph), and a staggering 54 gave no definition at all. There was even one article that used "neoliberalism" in the title but nowhere in the text. Rowlands and Rawolle thus urge critical educational researchers to use "the word 'neoliberal' and its variants consciously (indeed, reflexively) and critically in our research" (p. 270).

What precisely *is* this thing called neoliberalism? To work toward a definition, we call on literature that mobilizes "neoliberalism" as a gathering term for different changes that have taken place in international capitalism since the 1970s, but we also seek to locate these changes in a larger historical picture of the capitalist mode of production. In this way, neoliberalism is not presented as a radical break or departure from previous iterations of capitalism but as a particular phase of—or strategy within—capitalism. David Harvey's oft-cited work on neoliberalism helps to do just that. Although the picture of neoliberalism that Harvey paints is not without limitations—and, in the case of China, some mystifications—he presents a compelling definition of neoliberalism as a class strategy *within* capitalism. Based largely on the work of Gérard Dumènil and Dominique Lévy, Harvey (2005) argues that neoliberalism is "associated with the restoration or reconstruction of the power of economic elites" (Harvey, 2005, p. 19). The theoretical origins of neoliberalism can be traced back to a series of debates that took place in the 1920s–1930s over the role of the government in economic and political crises of the time. The theories began to be centralized in 1947 with the founding of the Mont Pelerin Society, whose most notable members included Thomas Hayek and Milton Friedman. The purpose of the society—which was named after the spa

UNIVERSITY OF WINCHESTER
LIBRARY

where its meetings were held—was to revive the study of free-market policies in response to Keynesian economic policies in the capitalist countries and the ascendancy of the Soviet Union and socialism after World War II.

Harvey locates the rise of what we might call "actually existing" neoliberalism in the years 1978–1980, which witnessed monumental events that took place at varying locations with a similar logic, sometimes coincidentally and sometimes not. The first event he points to is the ascendancy of Deng Xiaoping (and the rest of the eight elders) in China in 1978, after the death of Mao Zedong and the arrest of the "gang of four," a group of leaders in the Chinese Communist Party during the revolutionary Mao era. Deng and his associates initiated a series of economic reforms in China that "liberalized" China's economy, opening up space for private property, competition, and some (heavily state-sanctioned) foreign capital flows. This was a gradual—if uneven—dismantling of the key aspects of China's socialist economy, the four pillars being central planning, the absence of private property, collective ownership of land, and absolute state monopoly on foreign trade and investment. The second event that Harvey points to is the appointment of Paul Volcker to the position of chairman of the board of governors for the Federal Reserve System in the U.S. The "Volcker shock" was a monetary policy aimed at fighting inflation by increasing the federal interest rate, which sent unemployment figures skyrocketing. The third event, which accompanied this, was the election of Ronald Reagan in the U.S. in 1980. Reagan extended Volcker's monetarist treatment into the political and social sectors, particularly in regard to fighting the power of labor unions, implementing generalized deregulations of industry, agriculture, and finance. The final event was the election of Margaret Thatcher in Britain in 1979, who carried out a similar economic and political agenda to that of Reagan.

To what were these key events responses? In the case of China, which was quite distinct, Harvey mentions that the Deng reforms aimed "to amass wealth and upgrade its technological capabilities" to protect itself from internal and external threats, "to project its power outwards" and to prevent "the formation of any coherent capitalist class power bloc within China itself" (pp. 122–123). In the U.S. and Britain, however, the neoliberal turn arose in response to the growing political and economic threats over the rate of exploitation posed by organized labor and the new social movements of the 1960s–1970s. These movements were strengthened in the aftermath of World War II as a result of the "capital-labor" compromise. As a result of rising productivity—and capital realization—in the U.S. and Britain after the war, organized labor (representing primarily white workers) was able to negotiate higher shares of the values produced in the production process. In addition to the power of organized labor and the surplus labor-time they were able to reclaim, there were a host of social and revolutionary movements stirring. In his analysis, Harvey implies that neoliberalism was a capitalist class strategy within industrialized states and developing states and does not pay much attention to the broader global class struggle. The important point, however, is that there was an "*economic* threat to the position of ruling classes [that] was now becoming palpable" (p. 15). Neoliberalism, then, was about disciplining these movements, particularly when the economic crises of the 1970s emerged. This disciplining takes place through "deregulation, unrestricted access to consumer markets, downsizing, outsourcing, flexible arrangements of labor, intensification of competition among transnational corporations, increasing centralization of economic and political power, and finally, widening class polarization" (McLaren and Farahmandpur, 2001, p. 137).

Accumulation by Dispossession

One of the key aspects of neoliberalism for Harvey is "accumulation by dispossession." This language refers to Marx's concept of primitive—or, really, *primary*—accumulation, which comprises the last part of the first volume of *Capital*. Marx (1867/1992) here is taking up and criticizing the bourgeois political economist's story of the origins of capital accumulation (hence he titles this part of the book "so-called primitive accumulation"). The "origin" story told by bourgeois political economy is as follows: once upon a time (when, we are not exactly sure)

> there were two sorts of people: one, the diligent, intelligent, and, above all, frugal elite; the other, lazy rascals, spending their substance, and more, in riotous living... Thus it came to pass that the former sort accumulated wealth, and the latter sort had at last nothing to sell except their own skins. (p. 667)

In radical contrast to this bourgeois origin story, Marx demonstrates that it was, in actuality, "conquest, enslavement, robbery, murder...[and] force" (p. 668), which were the primary mechanisms through which the initial expansion of capital—and the conditions necessary for expanding capitalist production—were produced and accumulated. Toward the beginning of the first volume of *Capital*, while explaining the emergence of capitalism, Marx notes that the means and process of production under feudalism were nearly identical under early capitalism. The shift from feudalism to capitalism was, initially, a subtle shift.

Marx lays all of this out quite clearly in volume 1 of *Capital*. At its most basic economic level, aside from religious, state, and legal transformations, capitalism emerged out of feudalism with a subtle yet profound shift from feudalism's form of simple exchange (i.e., C—M—C) to capitalism's more advanced form of circulation where *money begets money* (i.e., M^1—C—M^2). As the division of labor developed under feudalism, a system of simple exchange became necessary to facilitate the distribution of useful products because a tailor cannot eat pants and a farmer cannot wear wheat. Simple exchange begins with a portion of the producer's product, which is exchanged for an equivalent value in the form of money and then exchanged for an equivalent sum of another producer's product for consumption. No new value is created in this process, which is why the production of use-values is dominant. The feudal lords' accumulation of the producers' surplus labor was therefore limited by direct local consumption. The initial emergence of capitalism did not require, as a prerequisite, the demise of the feudal lords. Unlike feudalism that begins with the producer's product (and mercantilism that begins with the merchant's pocket, his money, which is advanced for an equivalent sum of commodities, and then sold dearer), capital properly begins with the capitalist setting into motion the means of production and labor-power and, in the process, producing surplus-value:

> As the conscious representative of this movement, the possessor of money becomes a capitalist. His person, or rather his pocket, is the point from which the money starts and to which it returns. The expansion of value, which is the objective basis or main-spring of the circulation M—C—M, becomes his subjective aim, and it is only in so far as the appropriation of ever more and more wealth in the abstract becomes the sole motive of his operations, that he functions as a capitalist, that is, as capital personified and endowed with consciousness and a will…The restless never-ending process of profit-making alone is what he aims at. (Marx, 1867/1983, pp. 152–153)

The movement from feudalism to capitalism, of course, does not end there; capitalism is a necessarily expanding and developing system (although it is certainly not linearly so). There are three interrelated presuppositions on which a more advanced industrialized capitalist development production rests: first, a mass of people (workers) are separated from the means of subsistence (e.g., agricultural producers are expropriated from the land), which does not necessarily have to have happened for the master craftsman to become a capitalist; second, there is a need for commodities (i.e., the creation of the market) due to a highly developed division of labor, which existed in feudalism as a necessary prerequisite for the emergence of capitalism; third, there is a con-centration of resources, raw and ancillary materials, and primary means of production in the hands of one class. These three components are each part of the establishment of the capital-labor class relation/antagonism. Marx, it has been argued, portrays primitive accumulation as something in the past, something that laid the foundation for capitalist production and accumu-lation and then vanished into history. However, in Chapter 26 of volume 1 of *Capital*, Marx summarizes the process of expanding capital as cyclical, suggesting that primitive accumulation, rather than a one-time occurrence, is an ongoing necessity of the perpetually expanding property of capitalism. Consider:

> ...the accumulation of capital presupposes surplus-value; surplus-value pre-suppos-es capitalistic production; capitalistic production presupposes the pre-existence of considerable masses of capital and of labor-power in the hands of producers of com-modities. The whole movement, therefore, seems to turn in a vicious cycle, out of which we can only get by supposing a primitive accumulation...preceding capitalistic accumulation; an accumulation not the result of the capitalistic mode of production but its starting point...The capitalist system pre-supposes the complete separation of the laborers from all property in the means by which they can realize their labor. (pp. 667–668)

What Marx is getting at here, alluded to above, is an analysis that runs throughout the entirety of *Capital*, which treats primitive accumulation—like every other aspect of capitalism—as something that emerges not all at once but developmentally, through cycles that lead to different stages (such as the movement from manufacture to the industrial machine factory). For this reason, Marx goes on to argue that "as soon as capitalist production is once on its own legs, it not only maintains this separation, but reproduces it on a continually expanding scale" (p. 668). Also accompanying the histori-cal development (i.e., expansion) of capital has been periodic crises, which capital has traditionally exploited to realize more closely its internal drive, which is the fullest possible extension of capital's rate of exploitation even though that inevitably leads to the premature exhaustion and death of the laborer.

Several Marxist revolutionaries and scholars have done important work on *ongoing* processes of primitive accumulation. Most notably, Rosa Luxem-burg (2003) in her seminal work, *The Accumulation of Capital*, argues that there is an organic connection between capitalist production/accumulation proper (the production of surplus-value via the exploitation of wage-labor) *and* primitive accumulation (via colonial policy, international loan systems and payments of interest, war, and so on). These represent two distinct forms of exploitation under capitalism. However, this does not suggest that there is more than one way to augment new value capitalistically. What this suggests, on the contrary, is that not even the portion of the working day that represents the value labor creates for its own reproduction, that is, what is necessary, is safe from expropriation. In today's neoliberal stage of capital's historical development, labor is increasingly living in what seems to be a permanent stage of poverty being forced to survive on less value than what is socially necessary to reproduce oneself for another day of existence. Marked by drastic cuts in wages and social programs such as health care and education, labor as a whole (especially the least privileged) is suffering both materially and intellectually. Working-class resistance, although at times more or less pronounced, has been a common characteristic of capital since its earliest stages of development.

Continuing Luxemburg's line of thinking into the present day, David Harvey (2005) writes of "accumulation by dispossession." He identifies this type of accumulation as a primary component of neoliberalism and delineates four comprising features: 1) the privatization and commodification of formerly public goods, assets, and services; 2) the rise of finance capital and the deregulation of financial mechanisms of trade and accumulation; 3) the creation and management of debt crises as levers of accumulation; and 4) redistribution of values via the state (e.g., corporate welfare). One of the reasons why accumulation by dispossession is so crucial for Harvey's conception of neoliberalism is because it is a primary way in which the power of labor is broken by the organized efforts of the capitalist class. The power of labor is attacked through the attacks on labor unions and union-organizing drives but also through the privatization of public goods and the general transfer of wealth from the working to the owning classes. What this represents, as mentioned above, is capital finding new ways to realize the deadly internal drive and intent that always exists within it but has been subjected to various manifestations of state-imposed regulations or restrictions.

One of the most blatant examples of accumulation by dispossession was the 2008 bank bailout, which was literally the largest transfer of money (some of which represented actually produced value; much, however, was fictitious) from the working class to the capitalist class, facilitated by the U.S.

state in a completely bipartisan agreement. In addition to a $700 billion bailout to the banks, the U.S. state gave "trillions of dollars more in loan guarantees and other benefits to the major banks, insurance companies and other corporations" (Becker, 2012, p. 3) that caused the global capitalist economic crisis, in which we are still mired. There were very few strings attached to this massive influx of largely printed money-wealth. Richard Becker relates the story of a reporter who called the major banks to follow up on how they had used the bailout money. He lists some of their responses:

> Thomas Kelly, JPMorgan Chase (recipient of $25 billion): "We have not disclosed that to the public. We're declining to."
>
> Kevin Heine, Bank of New York Mellon ($3 billion): "We're going to decline to comment on your story."
>
> Carissa Ramirez, Morgan Stanley ($10 billion): "We're going to decline to comment on your story." (ibid.)

The banks were allowed to make this choice because the bailout package did not require them to. Becker notes how absurd the absence of such requirement is when compared with any government grant that, say, a community group might receive. In these cases, the government wants to know where every single cent ends up, and if any money can't be properly accounted for, then it must be returned. What this represents is how the state, in bourgeois society, is part of the capitalist machine. But as the capitalist tends to view capital as the true path to freedom and equality, such outcomes hardly appear out of place in a society where capitalism and democracy are commonsensically viewed as one and the same.

Because the process of accumulating surplus-value is a process that is disguised by the money relation, that is, it is concealed beneath the surface of wages where it appears every hour of work is paid, Marx notes that not even capitalists are conscious of the existence of surplus-value. The capitalist, like capitalist-educated labor in general, sees no difference between constant capital and variable capital. That is, between raw materials and machinery, constant capital, named as such because it creates no new value, and the use of human labor-power, variable capital, so named because it is the one commodity able to produce the value of its own equivalent (i.e., the average cost to live for one day), and an extra or surplus-value (i.e., the amount of time worked beyond what is necessary) that fluctuates according to such factors as intensity, productiveness, etc. One of the consequences of conflating constant and variable capital is that the bourgeois economists' calculation of the rate of profit is highly skewed, concealing the actual more extreme rate of exploitation. Unaware of this inherent exploitation involved in the productive consumption of labor-power, the capitalist actually tends to believe his purchase of labor-power on the market is fair. At the same time, because the capitalist mindset tends to view labor as part of machinery and raw materials, he also tends to believe that labor is a resource he is entitled to, that is, that it "belongs to the capitalist" (Marx, 1867/1983, p. 577). Marx uses the example of the capitalist perspective on immigration as an example. Another example is the way in which educators, from pre-K through higher education, are also viewed as part of the educational machinery and thus as a resource management is entitled to use as they please.

> Capitalist production, therefore, of itself reproduces the separation between labor-power and the means of labor. It thereby reproduces and perpetuates the condition for exploiting the laborer. It incessantly forces him to sell his labor-power in order to live, and enables the capitalist to purchase labor-power in order that he may enrich himself. It is no longer a mere accident, that capitalist and laborer confront each other in the market as buyer and seller. It is the process itself that incessantly hurls back the laborer on to the market as a vender of his labor-power, and that incessantly converts his own product into a means by which another man can purchase him. In reality, the laborer belongs to capital before he has sold himself to capital. His economic bondage is both brought about and concealed by the periodic sale of himself, by his change of masters, and by the oscillations in the market-price of labor-power. (pp. 577–578)

As workers, we are conditioned to be happy when our efforts to sell our commodity on the market are successful. It is a bourgeois position to focus on the relative privilege of some workers over others. As professors, we are especially inundated with messages that would have us feeling guilty because of the privilege of our occupations, that is, because of the relative autonomy (always contested) we supposedly enjoy over our labor and over the hours of the day, and because of the modest wage many professors enjoy. Of course, the goal of any serious socialist pedagogy is the complete emancipation of labor from the economic bondage of capital. That is, our Marxist pedagogy does not argue that the end goal should be to reduce the rate of exploitation to a reasonable level, with the end goal being to elevate the quality of life of all workers to the status of the most privileged segments of the working class.

Individual Freedom? Ha Ha Ha!

Once capital's surface appearances are penetrated and its hidden mechanisms and drives are exposed, it can be properly understood as an inherently dehumanizing force that must be resisted and transformed into socialism, which, in some way, ends the process of accumulating and creating surplus labor-hours. Within this context, neoliberalism begins to reveal itself as an intensified form of class rule. When the elevation of human suffering within the logic of capital's drive to accumulate dollars is not limited by working-class resistance and state intervention through regulation, the potential for working-class resistance escalates proportionally. And we are still here limiting ourselves to transformations *within* states governed by the capitalist mode of production.

One of the main reasons why neoliberalism has been able to take hold is because of the ways in which its particular (and completely abstract) notions of individual freedom and liberty have permeated so many facets of society. The base is the "freedom" of the free market, meaning that it should be free from government intervention. This, of course, is something of an ideological mystification. For there can be no private property—and thus no free market—without the state *enforcement* of private property. In other words, there has to be an immense repressive apparatus to legislate and enforce the rights of private property and trade. Harvey (2005) writes that the state is needed insofar as it must maintain "those military, defense, police, and legal structures and functions required to secure private property rights and to guarantee, by force if need be, the proper functioning of markets" (p. 2). Yet this apparatus exceeds the nation state. We can perhaps see the paradoxical status of the relationship between the free market and the neoliberal order by looking at supra-national free-trade agreements. As Sam Marcy (1990) notes in relationship to the General Agreement on Tariffs and Trade, "What is the very existence of such an agreement as GATT but a form of restricting the freedom of trade?" (p. 8). Marcy notes that, at base, such trade agreements are "a way to include some countries and exclude others from a particular arrangement among the monopolistic groupings in the imperialist world" (ibid.).

While there is a necessity for state intervention into the economy (and this one thing puts the *neo* in neoliberal), and while the state still serves as a mediating institution between antagonistic classes and social groupings, there is nonetheless a prevailing emphasis on freedom. This includes "individual" freedom—the freedom to be exploited, the freedom from direct access to the means of production, but certainly not freedom from want or the freedom from external control or command. This emphasis on freedom is able to subsume different discourses, many of which might at first seem to be antagonistic to capital. As Harvey (2005) writes, this "foundational emphasis upon individual freedoms, has the power to split off libertarianism, identity politics, multiculturalism, and eventually narcissistic consumerism from the social forces ranged in pursuit of social justice through the conquest of state power" (p. 41). This abstract notion of freedom is able to tame and encompass a plurality of political, social, cultural, and economic trends without challenging or even acknowledging the freedom or capital to dominate, exploit, and dehumanize, on an extending scale, laborers (i.e., all those who rely on a wage to survive, from the most to the least privileged). This sheds additional light on the ways in which pedagogies that do not take political economy into consideration can be subsumed within and made to work to perpetuate capitalist economic and social relations.

Neoliberalism and the Global Class War: From Revolution to Counterrevolution, and Back Again?

Neoliberalism, like every previous stage in capital's development, has not taken shape uniformly across the globe. In other words, neoliberalism's push to free capital from the regulatory fetters from freely exploiting human labor-power and the accumulated totality of society's wealth has not been realized from country to country consistently. As such, an examination of actually existing neoliberalism must be attentive to a host of particularities. Not every nation-state that has taken the neoliberal turn has done so in the same way. For example, in Chile, neoliberalism was enforced through the military dictatorship of Augusto Pinochet (put in power through a CIA-led coup and backed by the United States). Chile was actually in many ways the testing ground of early neoliberal doctrines, leading Friedman to coin the phrase "Miracle of Chile." This certainly differs from the neoliberal turn in the U.S., Britain, and Sweden, which did not involve military coups or fascist dictatorships.

Because of the uneven development of neoliberalism in practice, it is imperative to acknowledge that there are numerous and important debates taking place about *how* neoliberalism should be utilized as a theoretical framework for understanding contemporary political, economic, and social relations.

Jamie Peck and Adam Tickell (2002), for example, have argued for the importance of "walking a line" (p. 381) between "overgeneralized accounts of a monolithic and omnipresent neoliberalism" and "excessively concrete and contingent analyses of (local) neoliberal strategies" (p. 382). In response to this, Kalervo Gulson (2007) has claimed that neoliberalism is best theorized as a bricolage (and not a binary), thereby viewing "the 'monolithic' and 'extralocal' aspects of neoliberalism as mutually constitutive" (p. 191).

In other words, "neoliberalism is [in many ways] a meta-narrative" (p. 179), but this meta-narrative is highly contingent upon the varied localized ways in which it is expressed in policy and practice. In fact, it may be more proper to speak of neoliberalism as a meta-narrative that itself is not homogenous, but rather depends upon its varied instantiations. Again, this is not a new phenomenon of capital, as demonstrated by Marx's (1867/1983) discussion of the history of the expropriation of the peasant proprietor from the soil paving the way for the expansion and extension of the capitalist mode of production: "The history of this expropriation, in different countries, assumes different aspects, and runs through its various phases in different orders of succession, and at different periods" (p. 716).

In order to continue to ask what precisely neoliberalism is without getting mired in the endless articulation of particularities or remaining at the surface through homogenizing these particularities, we want to offer a clarification of what neoliberalism is by placing it within the context of the global class war, that is, the historical development of capital. Marcy's conception of the global class war—and its component global class camps—is crucial, we believe, for properly understanding neoliberalism as a *global class strategy* and not merely a capitalist class strategy *within* capitalism; it provides a more accurate understanding of the forces to which neoliberalism was responding and of its overall strategy.

Sam Marcy, who was perhaps one of the most important and, unfortunately, ignored, U.S. communist theoreticians of the 20th century, formulated the concept of the "global class war" in a document addressed to the internal membership of the Socialist Workers Party in 1953 (and this laid the theoretical basis for a split with the Party later in the 1950s). In the document, titled "The global class war and the destiny of American labor," Marcy (1979) asks two questions, one of which is internal to the politics of the SWP and the other which holds greater relevance for the communist movement: "Is there an independent destiny for the American proletariat?" (p. 45). The answer, of course, is no, because the American laborer is not an independent social entity but part of an international working class. In other words, it is the in-creasingly transnational and global capitalist whose policies reflect a commit-ment to exploiting the labor of workers globally. Marx understood perfectly well that the existence of capital itself already implies a global system since its primary drive for surplus-value knows no limits. Marcy next turns to a quote from Lenin's *What Is to Be Done?*

> The whole of political life is an endless chain composed of an infinite number of links. The whole art of the politician consists in finding and taking firm hold of the link that is most difficult to take from you, the most important at the given moment and the one which best guarantees to you the possession of the whole chain. (Lenin cited in Marcy, 1979, p. 46)

Not only is the American working class a part of the link in the global polit-ical chain, it is a *decisive* link. Not only, then, is the American working class *not* an independent social entity, but it is "an inseparable and completely in-terdependent link… of an entire global class camp" (ibid.). Neoliberal policies are therefore designed to more fully exploit and dominate this global entity.

What is the global class war? While more generally, we can locate its emergence with the emergence of capital itself, in a more recent framework, however, Marcy locates the origins of the global class war in the Korean War. Korea was not a war between states or a war between the North (led by the Korean Workers' Party) and the South (led by the U.S. under the cover of the United Nations); it was rather a war between classes. Marcy argued that the American communists were as a whole late to this realization and that the bourgeoisie had long "regarded the war from an exclusively global viewpoint" (p. 47). On the one side of the global class war is the camp of imperialism, those states and forces of capital expansion. On the other side of the global class war was the camp of the proletariat, Marcy's class camp. This camp con-tains within it, of course, "properly" proletarian wage-laborers in industrial-ized and imperialist states. But there are four changes in the composition of the proletarian class camp that Marcy identifies: 1) it includes "unlike the previous epoch… the bulk of the oppressed peoples in the colonies and de-pendent countries," those "peasants, semi- and non-proletarian elements;" 2) it "has state allies, states where the working class, if not in a political sense, then certainly in a social and historic sense, holds the ruling power"; 3) the "deformity" of Stalinism is on its way out; and 4) it has new allies in China and Eastern Europe, and this particular change "so thoroughly undermined the foundations of the imperialist structure that it can virtually be said that the world relationship of forces has been definitely and irretrievably turned in favor of our camp" (pp. 46–47). The "Cold War," that is, was not about the U.S. versus the Soviet Union, it was rather a struggle between the classes, a struggle that often manifested itself as a battle between leaderships, states, or groupings.

Marcy's analysis helps us appreciate more fully the global context within which the "capital-labor" compromise in the advanced capitalist countries took place. Viewing the struggle of the U.S. working class as one link in the global chain, we see that the advances made by organized labor in one country were propelled and enabled by the global proletarian struggle. If it were not for the advances made by the proletarian camp in the Soviet Union, China, Korea, Cuba, and so on, then the status of the camp in the U.S. and Britain, for example, would be drastically different. Interestingly enough, critical race theorist Derrick Bell (1995) gives this analysis credence in relation to race relations in the U.S. and the 1954 landmark *Brown v. Board of Education* ruling. Asking why, after decades of ruling against the desegregation of public schools, the Supreme Court suddenly ruled affirmatively, Bell suggested that the decision was the result of political and economic factors, not altruistic ones. Situating the decision historically, Bell noted that it emerged after the de facto end of the Korean War and at the beginning of the Cold War. As communist and national liberation struggles were being waged in Asia, Africa, the Middle East, and Latin America, the U.S. recognized that continued legal racism would only fan the flames of revolution. In other words, the national liberation struggles of the third world, waged primarily by people of color, were more likely to turn to the Soviet Union than the U.S., given the notoriously racist state of the latter and the relatively progressive state of the former. This, of course, turned out to be the case, as *de jure* desegregation did not have a *de facto* translation.

We can see the period between 1945, after the end of World War II, and 1979–1980, the time identified by Harvey as the rise of neoliberalism, as a period of global revolution in which the proletarian class camp was on the offensive. There were revolutionary, indigenous governments in power in the northern part of Korea and Vietnam. After defeating the nationalists, the Chinese Communist Party took power in 1949. In addition, there were new socialist states in Yugoslavia, East Germany, Poland, Hungary, Bulgaria, Romania, Czechoslovakia, and Bulgaria. By 1950, two fifths of the world's population lived within countries governed by a communist party. This solidification of working-class power as an effective counterweight against U.S.

imperialism undoubtedly provided a major impetus for a wave of national liberation struggles across the world. To name just a few examples: In 1952, the Egyptian revolution brought the nationalist government of Gamal Abdel Nasser to power, officially breaking the country free from British colonialism. A revolution in Iraq in 1958 freed that country from the same form of oppressive rule. Kwame Nkrumah and his Convention People's Party had liberated Ghana a year earlier. The Cuban Revolution took place in 1959, overthrowing the U.S.-backed dictatorship and kicking out foreign corporations. Throughout the 1960s and 1970s, nationalist or socialist revolutions and coups continued to take place, including countries such as Syria, Libya, Ethiopia, Iran, Afghanistan, Angola, Mozambique, Nicaragua, and Guinea-Bissau. These movements depended on material, military, and ideological support from the Soviet Union and, in many instances, China.

At this point it might be objected that this story is too linear, too neat, too laudatory, in a word, too *modern*. There is certainly credence to these objections, for there was certainly not a linear global march toward progress. In terms of linearity, it is important to note that there were setbacks throughout this period. There was the CIA- and British-backed coup against Mohammad Mossadegh's nationalist government in Iran in 1953 and the overthrow of Salvador Allende's socialist government in Chile in 1973 that was already mentioned. In terms of the neatness of presentation, it should go without saying that revolutionary situations are messy, violent, and contradictory. And, just as neoliberalism has unfolded differently in different states, regions, and continents, so too have socialist and nationalist revolutions.

In terms of the laudatory nature of our remarks on this period, we will be a bit more defensive. We have, to be sure, not offered a nuanced appraisal of each and every revolution during this period, and such a task is outside the scope of this book. We are ready to admit that there were many mistakes, errors, and even crimes committed in the name of socialism and progressive nationalism. There are, however, a few caveats that are imperative to mention about any such defaults. First, the task of overthrowing a centuries-old social system and implementing an entirely new one cannot be an easy or seamless task. A revolution is not, Mao Tse-Tung (1966) said, "a dinner party, or writing an essay... it cannot be so refined, so leisurely and gentle, so temperate, kind, courteous, restrained and magnanimous" (p. 11), for revolutions are ultimately violent acts of insurrection. Added to this reality is the fact that these social systems had to develop in difficult and hostile circumstances. For example, after the success of the Russian Revolution of 1917, the U.S. sent in troops—13,000 by 1918—playing a counter revolutionary role for two years. All in all, 14 imperialist countries sent troops to fight against the first successful workers' revolution. The invaders, the U.S. in particular, worked together with the White Army forces loyal to the former Russian ruling class, which engaged in a sustained campaign of terror against the revolution. Summarizing the long-term effects of this military intervention, Blum (2004) comments:

> History does not tell us what a Soviet Union, allowed to develop in a "normal" way of its own choosing, would look like today. We do know, however, the nature of a Soviet Union attacked in its cradle, raised alone in an extremely hostile world, and, when it managed to survive to adulthood, overrun by the Nazi war machine with the blessings of the Western powers. The resulting insecurities and fears have inevitably led to deformities of character not unlike that found in an individual raised in a similar life-threatening manner. (p. 8).

In addition to threats and actions of military interventions, all states hostile to—or even just uncooperative with—imperialist forces suffer from political and social sabotage and economic blockades and embargos. It should be expected that new social systems would be characterized by deficiencies and errors, particularly when being birthed and developed in such hostile historical conditions. Thus, despite how insightful and significant left-wing critiques of the USSR and actually existing socialism (e.g., Hudis, 2012) are for envisioning and struggling for a post capitalist future, critiques of the Soviet Union's contradictions and failures should not be disconnected from the larger historical and global context from and in which they arose. The Bolshevik Revolution, after all, attempted to create socialism not out of a well-developed capitalist economy but out of an inefficient and highly conservative feudalism with its accompanying backward social relations. Rather than receiving much-needed support from Western powers, the USSR found itself under severe assault. William Blum (2004) situates the ultimate fate of the USSR in the post-WWII era in the following context: "the opportunity to build the war-ravaged world anew, to lay the foundation for peace, prosperity, and justice, collapsed under the awful weight of anti-communism" (p. 7).

Additionally, our claim is *not* that this revolutionary period, marked by the offensive of the global proletarian camp, was idyllic or perfect. It would be absurd to claim that these revolutionary movements and states were paradises, just as it would be absurd to argue for a return to these particular formations. Neither are we claiming that these socialist or national liberation movements achieved some sort of internal harmony among the entirety of the population. Once the former colonizers were kicked out, for example, it is not as if there were not still problems of sexism or, in the national bourgeois states, class antagonisms. Our claim is rather that, taken as a whole, this global trend represented a radical *advance* against the machinations of capitalism and imperialism. If we take any country that was liberated from colonialism or imperialism in this wave of struggles, we can witness drastic improvements in standards of living, literacy rates, life expectancy, and so on.

The global scene during the 1970s looked promising in many ways. Not only were there great struggles taking place across the world defeating imperialism, there were also burgeoning resistance movements in the United States. The Civil Rights Movement had blossomed into a Black Liberation movement. In this latter movement, the primacy of the international situation is very clear, for the most organized expression of this movement, the Black Panther Party, saw itself as a domestic expression of Marxism, Leninism, and Maoism. This link was also clear in the anti war movement, which quickly became anti-imperialist, as young people not only opposed U.S. military intervention in Vietnam but also actively supported Vietcong fighters. The tide turned, however, after the Iranian, Grenada, and Sandinista Revolutions of 1979. It is at this moment that imperialism launched a real counterrevolution, setting out to reverse the gains made by the proletarian class camp during the previous three decades. Thus, neoliberalism is not only a strategy to reassert the rule of the capitalist class against labor *within* capitalist states, as Harvey insists. Neoliberalism is part and parcel of a broader global class program against the power of the proletarian class camp, which again includes not only socialist states but also those states independent of imperialism.

Global Counterrevolution and the Class Character of China

One of the key factors that propelled this counterrevolution forward was the alliance formed between China and the U.S. in 1979. We have already touched on how, after the death of Mao, Deng liberalized China's economy, undoing some of the pillars of the state's socialist economy. What we want to do now is to offer a clarification of the historical and ongoing role of China in neoliberalism and the global class war. There is no doubt that the alliance between China and the U.S.—which was ultimately an alliance *against* the Soviet Union, Vietnam, and the Eastern Bloc—represented the desertion of China to the bourgeois camp. Ever since Deng and his supporters wrested control of the Communist Party of China in 1976, Deng had been upheld as a "reformer" by the imperialists and their press (save for the extreme right wing). Thus, when Deng accepted an invitation by then U.S. President Jimmy Carter for a series of talks between January 29 and February 13, 1979, this was seen as a potential opening, and not just the potential of opening China to capitalist investment and exploitation but an opening for the imperialist camp to launch its counteroffensive. Potentiality was turned to actuality when, 12 days after these talks ended, China officially invaded the northern part of Vietnam with 400,000 troops. This signaled a de facto military alliance between China and imperialism. What China got out of this alliance was, of course, access to the latest Western technologies and scientific developments, as well as foreign investments to boost production.

Does China's desertion to the side of the bourgeois camp mean that China is no longer socialist or that it is neoliberal? We believe that, while we should answer the first question with an unqualified "yes," the answer to the second question remains negative. China is no longer properly a socialist state, in that "public ownership, centralized planning and the monopoly of foreign trade" (Becker, 2008, p. 16) have been either destroyed or severely eroded. There is a bourgeois, owning class in China that lives by exploiting labor-power. As Brian Becker (2008) notes:

> The economic reforms instituted since 1978 have eviscerated many of the social insurance guarantees previously enjoyed by the workers and even more numerous peasantry. Basic social rights—healthcare coverage for all, the right to a job, free public education, affordable housing—have been severely cut back for millions. (p. 17)

While the pillars of China's socialist economy have been uprooted, and while capital has marched forward, displacing and ravaging China's working class and peasantry, it does not follow from this that China is a neoliberal state, as Harvey argues. To his credit, Harvey does pay attention to the particularities of China in neoliberalism. Yet on the cover of his oft-cited book, *A Brief History of Neoliberalism*, a picture of Deng sits sandwiched in between pictures of Ronald Reagan, Augusto Pinochet, and Margaret Thatcher, establishing something of a visual equation of these figures.

China is a contradictory social and political formation. There is private property, competition, foreign investment, economic and social inequality, and exploitation. Yet this does not mean that capitalism has the definitive upper hand in China. There are still many state firms and industries in China, enough to earn the condemnation of *The Economist* (2009, Nov. 12). In fact, the Chinese constitution both consecrates the logic of the free market *and* affirms the presence of central planning for social needs, as Article 15 reads, "The state practices economic planning on the basis of socialist public ownership... balancing... economic planning and the supplementary role of regulation by the market" (quoted in Thompson, 2008, p. 91). Furthermore, China's economic prowess tends to be greatly overexaggerated. In fact, China is still technically an underdeveloped country. As Zheng Bijian (2005) notes, "China remains a low-income developing country, ranked roughly 100th in the world. Its impact on the world economy is still limited." Bijian goes on to write that, according to China's own estimations, it won't be until 2050 that China will overcome the long legacy of colonialism and underdevelopment.

Power is also still held by a Communist Party, which has a membership of over 85 million people. Because of the principles of democratic centralism, which keep democratic debate internal to the Party, we are not privy to all of the different factions within the organization. Yet in order to maintain its power, the Party cannot turn its back on its entire social base, and so one can deduce that there must be significant socialist groupings within the Party. Actually, we have more than the powers of deduction. On July 12, 2007, an open letter to the Party's leadership, which was penned by 17 Party members, was circulated in advance of the 17th Party Congress. The letter called for a return to Marxist-Leninist-Maoist thought and offered specific recommendations to the Party's leadership, warning that if China's economic "reforms" are not abandoned, then "A Yeltsin-type person will emerge, and the Party and country will tragically be destroyed very soon" (Ma Bin et al., 2008, p. 108). This letter clearly attests to a left wing within the Party, one that is significant enough as to voice its criticisms publicly.

The U.S.-China alliance cemented in 1979 served to further isolate the Soviet Union and the Eastern Bloc from the world economy. That same year, the U.S. refused to ratify the Strategic Arms Limitation Treaty with the Soviet Union (referred to as SALT II, because the first treaty was also shot down by the U.S. in 1972). This pressure resulted in the ascendancy of Gorbachev to the rank of Secretary of the Soviet Communist Party in 1985. And this was the overall context for the dissolution and overthrow of the Soviet Union and the Eastern Bloc socialist states between 1986–1991. This period—a historic setback for the proletarian class camp and the general struggle of oppressed people—had nothing to do with aspirations for "democracy" or "freedom," as is taught in U.S. history textbooks (and, unfortunately, is parroted in much of the U.S. left). Or, perhaps to be more accurate, this period and the counterrevolutions across Eastern Europe was for democracy, but democracy for the capitalist class. Thus, what we have witnessed in the decades since the collapse of world communism has been the wide-scale expropriation of previously commonly held resources and industries by international capitalists. Michael Hardt and Antonio Negri (2009) correctly note that this development largely propelled neoliberalism: "a large portion of the 'generation' of wealth under neoliberalism," they write, "has been achieved merely by feeding off the corpse of socialism, in the former second world as well as the first and third, transferring to private hands the wealth that had been consolidated in public property, industries, and institutions" (p. 266).

The drive for the expropriation and accumulation of values was also enhanced by the fall of the Soviet Union. Without an effective counterweight against imperialism, many independent and socialist states found themselves under the immediate threat of military and economic attack. The economic blockades on Cuba and the Democratic People's Republic of Korea were immediately expanded. A new war was started against Iraq—first by military means, then by economic means, and then again by military means. Thousands of bombs were dropped on Yugoslavia, Bosnia, and Kosovo to break up the federation, sending the different nations within the federation into turmoil and chaos. Panama was invaded, and its president was kidnapped and taken hostage in a U.S. prison. This is the context in which the recent wars on Afghanistan, Libya, and Syria must be seen. The invasion of Iraq in 2003 was not the doing of George W. Bush but flowed naturally from imperialist policy since 1979. It is similar with the U.S.'s policies toward states such as Venezuela, Bolivia, Ecuador, Iran, Sudan, China, Ukraine, Zimbabwe, and Russia. All of the states targeted by the U.S. since 1979 have had one thing in common: they have all been socialist or independent (bourgeois-nationalist), and thus a thorn in the side of the imperialist camp. As Brian Becker (2013) argues, this thrust is oriented toward the "destruction of the independent states that emerged in the formerly colonized world which had managed to sustain their independent status from Western imperialism as a consequence of their economic and military ties to the USSR and the socialist bloc" (p. 25). The *tactics* used by the U.S. against these states (and against resistance movements that do not hold state power, like the Revolutionary Armed Forces in Colombia or the Zapatistas in Mexico) have differed over time and in relation to each other, but they are all part of the same *strategy*.

Conclusion: Becoming in the Global Class War

Critical pedagogy has to have an adequate understanding of the global rela-tionship of class and national forces as an ongoing historical development central to the spirit and intent internal to capitalist logic, and this under-standing has to be primary. If one examines the current neoliberalization of U.S. public schools outside of this context, then one will only have a partial and therefore inadequate understanding of the dynamics at work, the futures and lives at stake, and the potential for connecting domestic social struggles to the international global class war. For example, without taking into account capital's ability to thrive off of accumulation by dispossession through impe-rialist policies and wars, we cannot fully appreciate capital's ability to revive and strengthen its rate of exploitation after severe economic crises. This is one of the reasons why we believe we are still in a period of counterrevolution: just look at the ways in which the revolutionary energy of the "Arab Spring" was channeled quickly into reactionary ends that were fairly satisfactory with imperialist desires in the region. Critical pedagogues and revolutionaries in the U.S. also have a lot to learn from the historic and contemporary struggles of workers and oppressed peoples throughout the globe. Some of these lessons come in the form of grave mistakes that we seek to prevent, and others come in the form of triumphs from which we seek inspiration. We also have produc-tive alliances to forge internationally.

Moreover, unless critical pedagogy has a correct theoretical assessment of and practical approach to the global class war, we can end up acquiescing to imperialism and uniting with our class enemy. This is particularly dangerous in the U.S., a country in which patriotism, national chauvinism, and war propaganda have done such damage to social movements. The recent war on Libya provides an instructive example. Before the 2011 war against Libya, there had been a decades-long demonization campaign against the Libyan government and its leader, Muammar Gaddafi, as well as military attacks and several rounds of economic and political sanctions. Thus, when an armed uprising broke out against the government in 2011, many people and groups on the left in the U.S. completely capitulated to the imperialist camp. Becker offers a proper, if scathing, assessment of this situation:

> So, in the case of Gaddafi and Libya, parts of the left and the peace movement said, well, Gaddafi's rule was dictatorial, or he was a bizarre leader, or there was a violation of human rights… echoing all the arguments of the imperialists. Absent social pres-sure, all of the socialists in their meetings can make militant speeches to each other…

But will you go out into the public arena, when the public has been trained by the imperialists to say if you oppose a war in Libya, then you are an apologist for Gaddafi, for the demon? If you are not just fighting conservatives, but mainstream public opinion that has been poisoned by demonization, you have to be strong. Much of the left's betrayal of internationalism was nothing other than an exercise in cowardice, in accommodating to public opinion, imperialist-generated public opinion, but cloaked and masked in left rhetoric and human rights rhetoric. (B. Becker in Glazebrook, 2013, p. 35)

One of the main reasons that there was not a mass movement against the war on Libya, Becker shows, is that so much of the left and "peace" forces ultimately parroted the line of imperialism and united with imperialism against Gaddafi, the Libyan government, and the Libyan people. This was facilitated by patriotic propaganda that held the U.S. as "democratic" and Libya as a "dictatorship." We would argue that we have witnessed the exact same trend happen in regard to Syria and that it could very well happen in relation to the DPRK and Iran. We can compare this to the state of social movements in the 1970s, when the Black and Chicano liberationists and the left more generally forged active links with anti-imperialist movements and states across the globe. This is an area in which critical pedagogy could provide a productive, anti-imperialist intervention, yet this possibility rests upon an appropriate historical-materialist understanding of the global class war.

· 3 ·

BECOMING COMMUNIST IN THE GLOBAL CLASS WAR: CENTERING THE *CRITIQUE OF THE GOTHA PROGRAMME*

Introduction

A critical pedagogy of becoming in the global class war proceeds from the premise that the whole system of accumulating surplus labor-hours must be abolished through a series of stages developing out of the concrete conditions of currently-existing capitalism. Through a dialectical movement of negation, the future can be excavated from within the present. This is precisely what Marx sought to do in his *Critique of the Gotha Programme*, which is the focus of this chapter. Marx's *Critique* was written in a different historical era, yet it offers important guideposts for a critical pedagogy that is oriented beyond capitalism and toward communism. We do not mine this text in the absurd hope of finding the key to transition, as if capitalism was a stagnant system just waiting to collapse into a higher stage of productive social relations. We are instead concerned with the historical content, relevant points of antagonism with social democrats, and purpose of the text. Before turning to this task, we lay the theoretical groundwork necessary for understanding Marx's *Critique of the Gotha Programme* in relation to both its historical conditions and its position within Marx's overall body of thought. At the end of the chapter, we delineate six key components of a Marxist critical pedagogy of becoming: a recognition and rejection of anti communism; an orientation toward the totality of life; an insistence on the connection to global struggles against exploitation and oppression (which includes an evaluation of the class character of these struggles); the utilization of critical, rigorous concepts and formulations; the location of our project within the communist horizon; and the necessity of organization and the Party.

Communist Education from within the Present

The Gotha Programme was the program written for the Social Democratic Workers' Party of Germany in 1875 based upon the work of the Party's socialist co founder Ferdinand Lassalle, with whom Marx was fundamentally at odds. Throughout his critique, Marx highlights, with rigorous passion, the points in the program that were based on Lassallean principles. In his 1892 Introduction to his then famous short manuscript, *Socialism: Utopian and Scientific*, published in 1880, just five years after Marx's (1875/2002) *Critique of the Gotha Programme*, Engels offers an argument against Berlin University professor Dr. Duhring's influential, anti-Marxist approach to socialism. Engels (1880/2007) situates his (and Marx's) position within the historical context of the importance of articulating the parameters of what a socialist alternative to capitalism might be at a time when "the Socialist party in Germany was fast becoming a power" (p. 15). Engels, however, provides an outline of the periodization of capital extending far beyond Germany. Beginning with English feudalism, that is, the rising, "expansive" commercial power of the class that would become the capitalist class—the feudal middle class—became "… incompatible with the maintenance of the feudal system" and it "had to fall" (p. 27). In the process of manifesting their revolutionary role against feudalism, the bourgeoisie forged a temporary alliance with the peasant class, which would become the working class. The inherent contradictions between these two antagonistic classes would eventually lead to a long legacy of deepening bitter struggle between them that persists to the present moment:

> The industrial revolution had created a class of large manufacturing capitalists, but also a class—and a far more numerous one—of manufacturing workpeople. This class gradually increased in numbers, in proportion as the industrial revolution seized upon one branch of manufacturing after another, and in the same proportion it increased in power. This power is proved as early as 1824, by forcing a reluctant Parliament to repeal the acts forbidding combinations of workmen. (p. 36)

Engels goes on to discuss such concessions (i.e., *combinations of workmen or unionism*) the working class, conscious of their own size and thus power, forced upon the capitalist class. In today's period marked by the generalized and global crisis of capital, such concessions are a thing of the past, but the need for a viable, theoretically sound socialist vision is particularly urgent. For example, István Mészáros (2011) argues that the current crisis of capital, unlike previous crises marked by distinct periods of growth and recovery, such as the Great Depression followed by the post-WWII boom era, is not *cyclical* but *systemic* and thus far more serious and permanent, ultimately threatening the survivability of humanity and the natural ecosystems more generally.

Again, because it was written as the guiding statement for Germany's socialist movement, and because in our current era, we too need programs for guiding movement out of capital, Marx's (1875/2002) position offers key insights that can assist laborers in general and educators in particular toward these ends. It should be noted that the whereabouts of Marx's original text is unknown. Perhaps it was destroyed. The text we *do* have is of an unknown handwriting, which Engels published in 1891. Despite this unfortunate circumstance, the text Engels published has been widely treated and regarded as Marx's original text.

The Historical and Theoretical Location of Marx's Critique

Engles's argument against utopian socialists offers an important analysis to help situate Marx's (1875/2002) critique in a contemporary context. For example, Engels (1880/2007) argues that the utopians' response to the immiseration engendered by early capitalism demonstrated their lack of understanding of the internal logic of capital. Consider:

> The socialism of earlier days certainly criticized the existing capitalistic mode of production and its consequences. But it could not explain them and therefore could not get mastery of them. It could only simply reject them as bad. The more strongly this earlier socialism denounced the exploitation of the working class, inevitable under capitalism, the less able was it clearly to show in what this exploitation consisted and how it arose. (p. 70)

Contemporary critical pedagogy, without Marx, suffers from exactly this shortsightedness. Because mainstream critical pedagogy and some of its

UNIVERSITY OF WINCHESTER
LIBRARY

post-structural variants begin by rejecting Marx, critical pedagogy tends to be based on simplistic understandings of social class that stress the consequences of capitalism, such as poverty, inequality—and, in education, educational inequality—without grasping the internal logic and driving force of capitalism. Marx lays this out clearly in volume 1 of *Capital*. As we noted in the previous chapter, at its most basic level, capitalism emerged out of feudalism with a subtle yet profound shift from feudalism's form of simple exchange (i.e., C—M—C) to capitalism's more advanced form of circulation where *money begets money* (i.e., M^1—C—M^2). As the division of labor developed under feudalism, a system of simple exchange became necessary to facilitate the distribution of useful products, because a tailor cannot eat pants and a farmer cannot wear wheat. Simple exchange begins with a portion of the producer's product, which is exchanged for an equivalent value in the form of money, and then exchanged for an equivalent sum of another producer's product for consumption. No new value is created in this process, which is why the production of use-values is the primary focus. The feudal lords' accumulation of the producers' surplus labor was limited by direct local consumption. The initial emergence of capitalism did not require, as a prerequisite, the demise of the feudal lords. Unlike feudalism that begins with the producer's product (and mercantilism that begins with the merchant's pocket, his money, which is advanced for an equivalent sum of commodities, and then sold dearer), capital properly begins with the capitalist setting into motion the means of production and labor-power and, in the process, producing surplus-value.

According to Marx, what the bourgeois economists and socialists did not fully comprehend was the logic behind the *appearance* that money can create more money within a market system based upon the theoretical or ideological exchange of equivalents. That is, money serves the role of exchanging products of various qualities (i.e., pants into bread or, to use one of Marx's examples, a bible into whiskey) into a certain quantity of a common denominator (i.e., labor hours) so they can be traded. If the law of the market is based upon the theory of fair exchange, then how does the merchant or industrialist consistently and systematically augment capital and become a capitalist? That is, how is the exploitation of labor-power hidden within the process of production? Marx explains this by differentiating between constant capital and variable capital.

Constant capital is the means of production and raw and auxiliary materials. He calls them constant because they create no new value—the value put in is roughly the same value that comes out (save a portion of the raw material that might be wasted through the production process itself or that is lost through general wear and tear, etc.). Variable capital, on the other hand, stands for the value of labor-power as represented through the wage (which is the price of labor-power and will fluctuate in relation to labor-power's actual value). It is labor-power that produces all values, including the value of the means of production and raw and auxilliary materials used in the production process. Labor-power, when set in motion and combined with constant capital to produce useful products, has the ability to create more value than what was advanced to purchase its use—but how? Labor-power adds value in two ways: first, by transforming the elements of production into a commodity (congealed labor-power); second, by preserving the value of the means of production.

Commodities have both use-values and exchange-values. Use-values are concrete, objective entities. Exchange-value, on the other hand, is immaterial and therefore social. Under simple exchange, a commodity's exchange-value serves primarily the function of facilitating the distribution of use-values. Money arises precisely as a means of exchange to lubricate this process. The deceptively subtle shift in capitalism, on the other hand, subordinates commodities' use-values to their exchange-value. For example, in *Seventeen Contradictions and the End of Capitalism*, David Harvey (2014) reflects on the tendency toward crisis that results from the ways in which use-value and exchange-value are "at odds with each other" (p. 15). Harvey uses the example of a house, whose use-values are endless, from raising a family to engaging in illicit activities. But in order to access a house's use-values, a certain amount of exchange-value, in the contemporary world, tends to be required. In the case of speculators investing in the fluctuating values of housing for the appropriation of exchange-value (i.e., profit), the use-value of housing can be subverted for millions of people. Harvey thus notes that "in the recent property market crash in the United States, about 4 million people lost their homes through foreclosure. For them, the pursuit of exchange-value destroyed access to housing as a use-value" (p. 21). Harvey expands this analysis and observes that "the same thing happens to health care and education (higher education in particular) as exchange-value considerations increasingly dominate the use-value aspects of social life" (p. 23). While commodities, such as houses and college degrees, are wealth, it is not labor alone that creates commodities. As a commodity itself, labor capacity has both a use-value and an exchange-value:

> At first sight a commodity presented itself to us as a complex of two things—use-value and exchange-value. Later on, we saw also that labor, too, possesses the same two-fold nature; for, so far as it finds expression in value, it does not possess the same characteristics that belong to it as a creator of use-values. I was the first to point out and to examine critically this two-fold nature of the labor contained in commodities. (Marx, 1867/1983, p. 41)

This two-fold nature of commodities is what allowed simple exchange to develop with the division of labor. It is this two-fold nature that forms the basis of exploitation. Marx argues that the value of labor is determined by the average, minimum cost it takes to reproduce the laborer for another days work. Let's say, as Marx does, that it takes 6 hours of labor to reproduce the value of one's daily existence. Any additional hours of labor-power expenditure is surplus and consequently represents the self-expansion of capital. This is the distinction between the exchange-value of labor-power (the wage) and the use-value of labor-power (the total laboring capacity during any given amount of time).

The "magical" expansion of value that occurs when the circulation equation of feudalistic simple exchange is reversed from C—M—C (commodity, money, commodity), which does not imply "a change in the magnitude of value" (p. 158), just a transformation of form, to M—C—M (money, commodity, money), cannot be explained by circulation or distribution. That is, shifting around the value that has already been created does not explain where value comes from. Again, what this suggests is that value cannot be augmented or expanded in circulation, and it cannot be augmented without circulation or without coming into contact with other buyers and sellers of commodities. However, the commodity that the laborer has to sell is the most essential commodity to the capitalist because it is the one commodity that is endowed with the capability of self-expanding value, as explained above. If the capitalist received no more value for the purchased labor-power than what is represented by his investment, then no expansion of value would occur. That is, if the laborer only worked as long as it takes to reproduce his or her own existence, no new value would be created.

If expended human labor deposited within useful products as a result of the labor process is the true source of capital's self-expansion, then, as a result of this never-ending chain of transactions, capital *consumes* labor. Labor-power is consumed in the production process; through this, it is set in motion, that is, compelled to work and thus expend itself, to use itself up, transferring its own subjectivity into the objects of production. The labor process is a process of productive consumption in which labor and materials are consumed as a result of working. Individual consumption is distinct from productive consumption. Individual consumption is a means of survival with the result being the consumer, a mere expenditure or using up of existing value. Productive consumption, on the other hand, has as the result "a product distinct from the consumer" (p. 183), and the goal is self-expansion. In individual consumption, the act of consumption is a finality, while in productive consumption, self-expansion is potentially endless.

In the labor process the laborer's labor is constantly in a state of transformation. Before being purchased or before the capitalist employs the laborer on credit (to be paid after the labor act is complete), the laborer is still; the act of laboring is a potential. Once set in motion, the laborer's potential to labor is now labor in action. Gradually, the labor in motion becomes motionless as it becomes embodied in a use-value, "the thing produced" (p. 189). The teacher, when teaching, is consuming, expending, or using up her labor-power. At the end of a period of education, the educator's labor capacity becomes motionless and embodied within the now educated or credentialized students or particular useful forms of labor-power. This process is essentially the same regardless of whether the educator is laboring in a public system and producing future laborers and thus future value or is laboring in a privatized system where their labor is creating both future labor-power and thus indirect value, and direct value as a service consumed by laborers seeking to increase the value of their labor capacity.

Because of the self-expansive quality of labor-power represented within the notion of variable capital, there exists a rate of exploitation or the rate at which capital is augmented. Marx observes that this ratio is determined by dividing surplus-value by variable capital, which he calls the "rate of surplus-value" (p. 216). However, how bourgeois economists calculate the rate of profit by combining constant capital and variable capital, significantly downplaying and diminishing the rate of exploitation that tends to exist within capitalist production, due, in part, to the cut-throat competition between capitalists, each striving to increase his respective rate of profit by any means necessary. In this way, capitalism is actually mystified for capital *and* labor, as Marx (1894/1981) writes in the third volume of *Capital*: this appearance "completely conceals the true nature and origin of profit, not only for the capitalist, who has here a particular interest in deceiving himself, but also for the worker" (p. 268). The working day consists of two elements, the first, that portion of the day that goes toward what is necessary to reproduce the value of keeping oneself alive to work another day, and the other part of the day, surplus labor, which comprises the basis of the creation of new value, as outlined above. Socially necessary labor is the result of historical and moral elements (i.e., class struggle). The struggle over the working day is a struggle over the values produced and to whom, or more accurately, which class, these values will accrue.

The capitalist's compulsion to extend the working day in absolute and relative terms is, from the perspective of the capitalist, fair and in compliance with the laws of market exchange (i.e., the exchange of equivalents), reasons Marx (1867/1983), because the value of labor-power is assumed to be based upon the average amount of labor hours it takes to reproduce the laborer's physical, objective existence (i.e., the share of social product, or social wealth, needed to keep the laborer alive for another day), and the capitalist, it is assumed, pays this amount to the laborer in exchange for his labor. However, because the laborer is compelled to work beyond the time it takes to create the value to replace her own existence, from her perspective, she is being cheated out of her own surplus labor. Since both parties, the capitalist and the laborer, have legitimate claims within market logic, and since the interests of labor and capital are antagonistically related, Marx notes that ultimately, "between equal rights force decides" (p. 235). Summarizing the view of labor here regarding these two mutually exclusive perspectives, Marx offers a key insight for our critical pedagogy of becoming:

> The commodity that I have sold to you differs from the crowd of other commodities, in that its use creates value, and value greater than its own. That is why you bought it. That which on your side appears a spontaneous expansion of capital, is on mine extra expenditure of labor. You and I know on the market only one law, that of exchange of commodities. And the consumption of the commodity belongs not to the seller who parts with it, but to the buyer, who acquires it. To you, therefore, belongs the use of my daily labor power. But by means of the price that you pay for it each day, I must be able to reproduce it daily, and to sell it again…I will each day spend, set in motion, put into action only as much of it as is compatible with its normal duration, and healthy development. By an unlimited extension of the working-day, you may in one day use up a quantity of labor power greater than I can restore in three. What you gain in labor I lose in substance…You pay me for one day's labor-power, whilst you use that of three days. That is against our contract and the law of exchanges. I demand, therefore, a working day of normal length, and I demand it without any appeal to your heart, for in money matters sentiment is out of place. You may be a model citizen, perhaps a member of the Society for the Prevention of Cruelty to Animals…; but the thing that you represent face to face with me has no heart in

its breast. That which seems to throb there is my own heart beating. I demand the normal working-day because I, like every other seller, demand the value of my commodity. (pp. 233–234)

It is critical to note that this is where the laborer is introduced as being poised against capital—poised not yet as a revolutionary agent but as a voice for fairness within the laws of exchange, which implies the exchange of equivalents. This approach fits within Marx's dialectical conception of historical change as a developmental process. Capitalism, that is, did not magically appear as feudalism vanished but developed out of the social and economic structures that existed, as perpetually developing entities, within feudalistic society (with, of course, a violent process of primitive accumulation, a struggle over the state, etc.). The paradigmatic shift from exchanging commodities for money to access other commodities for consumption to exchanging money for commodities for money first emerged within the means of production and division of labor as they existed in late feudalism. Marx's place of departure for developing a theory out of capital necessarily begins with the exploitation of the laborer, which could not be done until the secret of how value is augmented through capital's M—C—M circulation process was uncovered.

The longer the capitalist can compel the laborer to labor beyond the time it takes to reproduce her own existence, in other words, the higher the rate of the capitalists' return on his labor-power investment. The longer the laborer works, the more value absorbed by raw material and subsequently transformed into useful products. When these values are compared, what is revealed is the rate of exploitation. If the value of labor and the value it creates are equal, then no new value would have been created. But new value is created and stored within the bodies it is transferred into. Once sold on the market, its value is finally realized, and money has been transformed into capital and accumulated as such, adding more value to the sum of capital to be invested to continue the process of self-expansion. The laborer, as a consequence of not having direct access to the means of production, has to exchange her labor for a wage to survive and thus trembles when no buyer can be found. However, the more the laborer labors, the more surplus-value his labor creates, thereby increasing the wealth and thus domination of capital over the producer and the production process.

However, it is important to stress that the shift from feudalism's simple exchange to the insatiable drive to accumulate surplus-value represents perhaps an even more subtle, yet profound, shift than has yet been suggested.

Fundamental to this shift is the fact that "capital has not invented sur-plus-labor" (p. 235). Surplus labor is present in any society where a "part of society" owns the greater part of the means of production, and laborers, "free or not free," must provide the "working time" necessary for their own "maintenance" and "extra" labor hours for the "maintenance" of the "own-ers" (p. 235).[1] The difference resides in the fact that only in capitalism is the commodity's exchange-value given primacy over its use-value. In feudal-ism, for example, the accumulation of surplus labor-hours was limited by how many use-values could be consumed by the laborers and by the feudal nobility/owners. In pre-capitalist societies, laborers are therefore rarely over-worked or worked to death, because production itself without consumption does not foster "a boundless thirst for surplus-labor" (p. 235). The exception was when labor was directed at producing "exchange-value in its specific independent money-form; in the production of gold and silver" (p. 235). In other words, Marx notes that before the capitalist era, the only example of laborers being worked to death was in the mining of gold and silver, which is basically the process of digging up money or direct exchange-value. In a later chapter, we examine how this process worsens slavery and exacerbates racism.

The transformative property of variable capital, activated by the raising or lowering of the length of the working day (regardless of what unit of mea-sure the capitalist employs, such as the hourly wage, the yearly wage, or the daily wage) necessarily remains hidden below the surface *operating behind the backs of producers*, as it were. This is so because "surplus-labor and necessary labor glide into one another" (p. 236). This more or less hidden flexibility of variable capital has over time proven to serve the capitalist well during times of crisis. That is, when business is bad, the length of the working day can be extended through various measures such as lowering the hourly wage, forcing, in effect, laborers to work more hours to reproduce their own existence. It is not uncommon for wages to be suppressed to below basic subsistence lev-els, or below what is necessary to replace what was expended during the labor process. During such times of crisis, which now seem to be the normal, permanent state of late-capitalism, laborers become more and more aware of how they are being exploited. The surface appearance of poverty next to opulence is not hard to detect. What is more difficult to uncover is the specific way value is augmented capitalistically, how it emerged historically, and what it might develop into provided a sufficiently critically conscious working-class agency.

The Critique of the Gotha Programme and Critical Pedagogy

As with the socialists critiqued by Marx and Engels, critical pedagogy today focuses on the readily visible consequences of capital (i.e., issues of exchange and distribution) without grasping its internal logic, which plays a *structurally determining* role in its historical development. Paula Allman, Peter McLaren, and Glenn Rikowski (2005) have referred to this as the "box-people" approach. In this approach, social class is determined by checking boxes with varying levels of income, consumption power, social status, and so on. The focus on the consequences of capital also fails to grasp the hegemonic and counter hegemonic manifestations of human agency mediating capital's transformation through time and space. Again, Marx's body of work offers crucial insights for correcting these shortcomings. However, as suggested above, contrary to Marx's time, capitalism today is in a descending phase, which requires some updating. Despite this disclaimer, the key insights and arguments of Marx (and Engels) remain relevant. Within the context of the savagery of capitalism's internal logic and drive that Marx so painstakingly uncovers in *Capital*, his *Critique of the Gotha Programme* as pointing to a post capitalist future takes on its full urgency and vitality.

Marx's critique is thorough, systematic, and relentless. He begins his assault attacking the program's very first sentence that claims that *labor is the source of all wealth*. In response, Marx argues that:

> Nature is just as much the source of use values (and it is surely of such that material wealth consists!) as is labor, which is itself only the manifestation of a natural force, human labor power. (p. 3)

What Marx is rallying against is an analysis that disconnects humanity, what we wrote about in Chapter 1, from the *production of the system of nature*. What is more, the entire basis for capitalistic wealth is based upon the expropriation of the laborer from the soil, from nature. That is, capitalism cannot function without a working class who have no direct access to land, to nature, and thus, out of necessity, must sell their capacity to work for a wage—one of the primary sources of both exploitation and permanent alienation. Relatedly, Marx (1875/2002) essentially charges the Gotha Programme with failing to break with bourgeois ideology:

The bourgeoisie have very good grounds for fancifully ascribing *supernatural creative power* to labor, since it follows precisely from the fact that labor depends on nature, that the man who possesses no other property than his labor power must, in all conditions of society and culture, be the slave of other men who have made themselves the owners of the material conditions of labor. He can only work with their permission, and hence only live with their permission. (p. 3)

What this points to is a critical pedagogy focused on developing a critical consciousness—an epistemological endeavor—and gaining control over one's creative capacities or labor-power—an ontological project—thereby ending the appropriation of surplus labor-hours, not as an end in itself but as part of the process of liberating the system of nature from the bourgeoisie's monopolistic control. With this in mind, it is worth reflecting on what this might mean for public education. In the spirit of showing students what this might look like in practice, it is not enough to challenge the neoliberal privatization of public education, as tends to be the focus in the United States, for it does nothing to subvert the way in which *the system of nature* is being held hostage against the majority and plundered for wealth extraction through the command and domination of society's collective labor-power (despite a long, ongoing tradition of working-class resistance). In Malott's experience working with a relatively small group of activist-educators employed by the Pennsylvania State System of Higher Education (PASSHE) who are active members of their union, the Association of Pennsylvania State College and University Faculties (APSCUF), it is a difficult task just convincing their colleagues on their own campus that privatization is neither good nor inevitable. The challenge of building a campus wide movement to challenge capital itself remains a daunting task.

However, the leap from challenging privatization, or the intensification of capitals' appropriation, to questioning the viability of capital is not a far one. The logic is simple enough: If more unrestricted capitalism is undesirable, then no capitalism must be best. If this is so, then what exactly is it about capitalism that is so unwelcome? And what might an alternative look like and how might we realize it? These discussions, touched on throughout this essay, can and should be had (see Hudis, 2012). In short, then, what exists as a countermovement to capital in the U.S. tends to be focused on resisting neoliberalism, but not capital itself. Again, putting the difficulty here in context, it is worth restating that building support for a movement against privatizing public education is not easy outside of small critical pedagogy and socialist circles. Marx's challenge for a socialist alternative represented in this chapter offers a vision of the future, properly articulated through a collective movement, we believe, would be widely accepted despite the many ideological challenges. For example, Noam Chomsky has made frequent reference to the fact that many Americans who self-identify with procapitalist politics, such as those associated with the Democrats, Republicans, and the Tea Party, when questioned on specific policy issues, actually support a program quite far to the left, including universal healthcare, livable wage mandates, and free universal education.

Outside of the United States, however, global neoliberal trends seem to be met with more resistance. Offering powerful insights and descriptions of the concrete context of neoliberal attacks on public education in Greece, the soil out of which the resistance movement there has grown, Leonidas Vatikiotis and Maria Nikolakaki (2013) explain:

> Under the Memorandum regime that requires the citizens of Greece to pay back an alleged and unscrutinized debt, social services such as education and health care have been significantly reduced...The aim is to make public education a free market...reduce curriculum to basic math and literacy content that workers will need to compete for low-paid jobs...This is part of a global project. Debt makes it seem inescapable...Targeting and scapegoating teachers is one of the means of neoliberalism in this global project...Taking the spirit out of the souls of the teachers is a primary goal of debtocracy. Cuts in education in Greece include cuts in teachers' salaries up to 40%. As a result, teachers are living at the edge of poverty and are demoralized. (pp. 142–143)

Vatikiotis and Nikolakaki, however, report many examples of teacher resistance despite an inability to push back crippling austerity measures. At the university level, however, students and professors have achieved some notable victories, despite some crushing losses:

> In Greece, education is free. All universities are public, and the privatization of higher education is forbidden by the constitution. Even so, the previous governments of Greece attempted to amend the constitution to allow for private universities and to facilitate a radical change in the framework of the public universities to allow private enterprises to fund public education. All of these plans failed because of the massive protests by students and staff that erupted in the spring of 2006 and the winter of 2007. It was a victory...as the government...still...cannot demand fees from students for higher education. (Vatikiotis & Nikolakaki, 2013, p. 145)

Through a series of intimidation tactics and political coercion in the face of massive student and faculty resistance, Greece's democratic university governance structure was radically altered, imposing corporate-dominated Administrative Councils charged with high-level decision making. Like elementary and secondary educators, university professors have also experienced the crushing blows of 40% budget cut situations. The response to the corporate take over and defunding of higher education in Greece was decisive, "more than 300 university departments were occupied by students for more than a month" (p. 150). While these massive actions were not able to reverse what was lost, they produced many experienced revolutionaries who will likely lead future campaigns. Additionally, at the time of this writing, SYRIZA, the radical left-wing alliance party in Greece, has achieved a fairly historic electoral victory, winning the position of prime minister. While the outcome of this development is yet to be seen (and is complicated by a similar rise in the fascist Golden Dawn grouping), it no doubt represents a continuation of these longer struggles over public use-values.

Strikingly similar courageous acts of resistance have flourished across the world. In Britain, for example, university students have responded to austerity with direct-action militancy. Consider:

> In early 2010, a handful of universities began to introduce cuts to particular departments and disciplines to which students responded. Perhaps most notable was the occupation of Middlesex University during April and May 2010 in response to the university's decision to close its philosophy department...Prior to autumn 2010 there were also strikes at London Metropolitan University, whose Vice Chancellor had claimed government funds for fictitious students; in response the university cut academic jobs and strikes ensued. (Canaan, Hill, & Maisuria, 2013, p. 183)

Given the global nature of capitalism, and thus the global nature of the crisis, we would expect to find resistance wherever austerity measures have cut public services, such as education. The situation is similar in Turkey, where:

> Neoliberal and neo-conservative education policies implemented after 1990 faced very significant resistance by dissident teacher unions, especially university students, academic staff and some political parties. It should be noted that this opposition was organized at the grassroots level, and was characterized by rigorous commitment to democratic principles. (Inal and Öztürk, 2013, p. 211)

Likewise but focused on Ireland, Michael O'Flynn, Martin J. Power, Conor McCabe, and Henry Silke (2013) make profound observations regarding the global financial crisis, its negative effects, and the existence of widespread resistance:

We draw attention to the nature of the Irish boom, to the specific character of the subsequent crash, highlighting the conditions that permitted the financial interest to effectively close ranks, transferring private debt to the general population. Whilst acknowledging the apparently low level of resistance to all of this, we reject the notion that the population has meekly accepted all of the related cuts and impositions. We show that the apparent submission to the austerity agenda is quite deceptive, that forms of resistance are emerging everywhere, not least in education, and that these represent the potential for the development of a mass movement against austerity in the years ahead. (p. 164)

A closer examination of the emerging movements around the world would surely reveal comparable sentiments regarding the existence of a similar mass movement simmering just beneath the surface of superficial consent. Activating this potential is the challenge of our critical pedagogy of becoming. Toward these ends, Vatikiotis and Nikolakaki (2013) summarize their vision for future resistance in Greece:

The most crucial area where this response will be judged is that of demands, which concentrates the political direction and the content of the struggle. Against this strategic attack of capital, there is an imminent need for a program of demands that could relieve the social majority. Each of these demands could be realized today under pressure from the social movements, but they cannot be realized as a whole while the demands exist as a radical program of claims and are not in synch with today's system. Their common character is that they challenge the power of capital; they are aggressive and they are in a position to improve the situation of the working and middle classes. These demands are: creation of payments and the abolition of the debt, exit from the Eurozone and the European Union, nationalization of banks and of firms of strategic importance, increases in wages, salaries, and pensions, and the empowerment of the public sphere. The adoption by the labor movement of these demands will determine the shape of how the Greek crisis develops. (pp. 151–152)

Such demands are a challenge to movements against neoliberalism to more centrally develop into movements against capital in general rather than against just certain manifestations of it. If recent examples of students taking over universities not only in Greece but in Quebec, Chile, and Mexico as well offer important tactical insights for physically *taking* buildings as a collective action, they must also be guided by larger visions that go well beyond the important goal of reversing trends in budget cuts and privatization. What Marx (1875/2002) seems to offer this discussion is that the seizing of land and buildings should not be viewed as a way to *only* force pro-labor reforms but as part of the process of subverting the basis of capital itself—the monopolization of nature, of land, of the means of production. The teaching of history here is fundamentally important. That is, to fully grasp the importance of land, a historical understanding of how capitalism has developed and spread through a process of primitive accumulation is crucial.

Also introduced here is the importance of critical geography and the understanding that space is socially produced and subject to the value dialectic (Ford, 2013). Space, in other words, must always be defined in relation to its useful effect, that is, whether it is being used to produce use-value or exchange-value (see Ford, 2014). The seizing of land and occupation of buildings by workers and students can thus potentially transform the use to which buildings are being put and thus their relationship to the capitalist mode of production's augmentation of value. For example, in 2014, Ford participated in a sit-in at Syracuse University, in which students occupied part of the main administration building for nearly a month to protest the ongoing privatization of the campus, including cuts to student services and scholarships for working-class and oppressed students. During the day, hundreds of students (graduate and undergraduate), staff, faculty, and community members stopped by for varying periods of time to speak, study, and organize. After 10 p.m. each day, around 40 students stayed in the building as it closed to sleep, collectively decide how to respond to the latest response by the administration, and continue organizing the movement. This building, in many ways the center of power of the corporate university, had been reclaimed and was being put toward other ends, useful not in relation to capital's needs but to the collective needs of the students.[2]

The next point that Marx (1875/2002) takes issue with relevant to the development of critical pedagogy is that "'the proceeds of labor belong undiminished with equal right to all members of society'" (p. 4). First and foremost, Marx argues that this statement "...has at all times been made use of by the champions of the *prevailing state of society*" (ibid.). That is, the capitalist class is the idle class, the class whose wealth and culture come from the labor of others. Stating that a society's productive output belongs, undiminished, to all member of society, leaves the privileged position of the non laboring bourgeoisie intact. Not only does the idle class represent a major strain on the *undiminished proceeds of labor* but so do the inevitable costs of maintaining and improving the instruments and providing insurance against unforeseen mishaps, mistakes, and natural disasters. The notion of *undiminished proceeds of labor*, for Marx, is nothing more than abstract jargon. From here, we might note that Marx is challenging us to ensure our critical pedagogy and program for action is free of loose concepts and uncritical rhetoric. For example, when we engage our critical pedagogy to challenge the policies of university administrators and governing boards, our analysis and goal should include the abolition of the non laboring (i.e., non teaching), bourgeois governing class, and thus the abolition of ourselves as externally controlled labor (i.e., professors, 70% of which in the U.S. are now part-time, contingent proletarianized, adjunct workers). True to his dialectical approach, the elimination of the unproductive administrative labor is conceptualized as a gradual process: "this part will, from the outset, be very considerably restricted in comparison with present-day society and it diminishes in proportion as the new society develops" (p. 7).

Marx then challenges the Programme for only challenging the capitalist class and not the landowners represented in their statement that "'the instruments of labor are the monopoly of the capitalist class'" (p. 5). For Lassalle wanted the party to form an alliance with the landowners at the expense of an alliance with the peasants. The importance of this insight, for Marx, resides in the fact that capitalists frequently do not own the land on which their factories are located. This critique reinforces our previous point, since university administrators at public institutions do not own the land on which the knowledge factories they operate are located. It is the state that owns the land, and the purpose of the state in the current era of global capitalism—an era marked not by cyclical crisis but by systemic and thus permanent and dangerous crisis—is to mediate and stall capital's current, structurally determined descending phase (Mészáros, 2011). Our critical pedagogy must therefore address not only all sectors of the capitalist class—including money capitalists, merchant capitalists, and commodity capitalists—but the landowning class as well, which is indispensable for converting *all* of the *instruments of labor* into society's *common property*. Moreover, this will help us be attentive to the internal contradictions of the capitalist class.

Engels's (1880/2007) discussion of the role of the state during the period of the historical development of capital not only remains relevant but also contributes to Marx's critique. For Engels, the state is "the official representative of capitalist society," and as the cyclical crises deepen and become permanent, and thus systemic, it "will ultimately have to undertake the direction of production" (p. 87). We have seen this tendency throughout the capitalist world, most notably as a response to the economic crisis of 2008, where banks and large automobile manufacturers were bailed out and temporarily taken over by various nation states from the U.S. to Great Britain. More concretely defining the role of the state within capitalism, Engels explains:

> The modern state, no matter what its form, is essentially a capitalist machine, the state of the capitalists, the ideal personification of the total national capital. The more it proceeds to the taking over of productive forces, the more does it actually become the national capitalist, the more citizens does it exploit. The workers remain wageworkers—proletarians. The capitalist relation is not done away with. (p. 88)

The austerity measures ravaging much of the world make the most sense in the context of Engles's notion of the state as a "capitalist machine." The No Child Left Behind Act, Race to the Top, and the War on Terror in the United States are obvious products of this machine. Such insights challenge the rallying cries in critical pedagogy for saving public education from the neoliberal era's movement to privatize the welfare state by challenging the state itself as a mechanism and tool of capital. While public spaces tend to offer more room for creative critical pedagogies, and, it might be argued, are worth saving, today's capitalism cannot return to that of previous eras. What is more, the extreme right-wing political parties argue that public education is socialism and must be freed from this monopoly so the most competitive products can rise to their market-determined place of superiority, allowing inferior competitors (i.e., schools) to perish. In this context, fighting for public education is a progressive position. For Marx, the state should fund education but have no control over its purpose or curriculum. As argued above, critical pedagogy needs a purpose and vision that can see beyond the social universe of capital (McLaren, 2005).

What comes next is a particularly heavy blow, as Marx (1875/2002) accuses the Programme of employing, "loose notions...in place of definite economic conceptions" (p. 6). This critique is directed, for example, at the previously mentioned statement that "'the proceeds of labor'" (ibid.) should be distributed equitably:

> What are "the proceeds of labor"? The product of labor or its value? And in the latter case, is it the total value of the product or only that of the value which labor has newly added to the value of the means of production consumed? What is "equitable distribution"? Do not the bourgeoisie assert that the present-day distribution is "equitable"?

These questions are relevant for critical pedagogy, as they challenge critical educators to fully think through what it means to fight for justice. Socialism, for Marx, does not stem from a redistribution of wealth but from subverting the process of accumulating surplus-value. Peter Hudis's (2012) book, *Marx's Concept of the Alternative to Capitalism*, brings together, for the first time, a comprehensive account of Marx's developing idea of what a postcapitalist future might look like by emphasizing what cannot exist (i.e., M—C—M) for capitalism to have been transcended. As we will see below, the focus on equitable distribution in a Marxist critical pedagogy is misplaced.

In his other works, Marx does not in fact call for equitable distribution but for the abolition of the generalizable, abstract equivalent, operating behind the backs of producers, which is necessary to begin transcending the root cause of alienation (i.e., the permanent and expanding separation of thinking and doing or mental and manual labor) under capitalism (and poverty and immiseration in the process). As Marx writes in the second volume of *Capital*: "If we were to consider a communist society in place of a capitalist one, then money capital would immediately be done away with, and so too *the disguises that transactions acquire through it*" (Marx, 1885/1978, p. 390, emphasis added). This analysis is particularly necessary for envisioning a human existence beyond the law of capital and the producer as commodity.

Marx then argues that the transition to socialism should not only see the proportion of wealth going to unproductive administrative labor decrease, but it should also see a greater portion of the proceeds of labor going to schools, healthcare, and other services designed to meet humanity's collective needs (contrary to the purpose of the capitalist state as argued above). In regard to education and other social services, Marx (1875/2002) notes that "from the outset this part is considerably increased in comparison with present-day society and it increases in proportion as the new society develops" (p. 7). In the current context of the new educational normal, that is, a perpetual, downward spiral of budget cuts and privatization, a greater emphasis on education to facilitate the process of collective becoming is not hard to imagine. Essentially, Marx is making the case that the very concept of the *undiminished proceeds of labor* is simply out of place and misguided in a postcapitalist society. Consider:

> Within the co-operative society based on the common ownership of the means of production, the producers do not exchange their products; just as little does the labor employed on the products appear here as the value of these products, as a material quality possessed by them, since now, in contrast to capitalist society, individual labor no longer exists in an indirect fashion but directly as a component part of the total labor. The phrase "proceeds of labor," objectionable even today because of its ambiguity, thus loses all meaning. (p. 8)

Put another way, we might say that the phrase "proceeds of labor" only makes sense (and for Marx, not very much sense) in the context of a capitalist society where laborers, as a general rule, do not consume or control the products of their own labor. That is, the concept hints at the separation among labor, commodities, and "proceeds." Marx is absolutely clear here as he reminds his readers that what he is alluding to is the development of communist society, which does not and cannot develop "'on its own foundation,'" as the Gotha Programme suggests, "but on the contrary, as it emerges from capitalist society; which is thus in every respect, economically, morally, and intellectually, still stamped with the birthmarks of the old society from whose womb it emerges" (p. 8).

Clearly Marx's concept of a postcapitalist society places human agency at the center, mediating the structural determinations of the capitalist mode of production. However, Marx has too often been interpreted as advocating a form of economic determinism. The passage presented earlier in this chapter where Marx is speaking from the perspective of the laborer, conscious of both her exploitation and capacity to challenge it, speaks to Marx's keen awareness of how capital operates according to an internal logic that can be either consented to or resisted. While capitalist society develops in a very specific direction, its future, for Marx, is not predetermined. Engels's (1880/2007) conception of social change has also been interpreted as economically deterministic. Consider the following rather lengthy passage from *Socialism: Utopian and Scientific*:

> The materialist conception of history starts from the proposition that the means to support human life and, next to production, the exchange of things produced, is the basis of all social structure; that in every society that appeared in history, the manner in which wealth is distributed and society divided into classes or orders is dependent upon what is produced, how it is produced, and how the products are exchanged. From this point of view the final causes of all social changes and political revolutions are to be sought not in men's brains, not in man's better insight into eternal truth and justice, but in changes in the modes of production and exchange. They are to be sought not in the philosophy, but in the economics of each particular epoch. (pp. 71–72)

From the perspective of bourgeois ideology this passage could be interpreted as advancing the idea that it is not humans that create change but the structural determinations of social systems working on their own, free of human intervention, like a clock wound up and moving through predetermined motions. However, situated in the larger context of Engels's argument against bourgeois utopian socialists, he is arguing that the critical human agency of the working-class is *not* informed by the superior intelligence of a few elite philosophers but by particular understandings and analyses of the *material conditions* that give rise to unmet needs. Because an analysis of the internal workings of capital is neither spontaneous nor does it come automatically from experience, it has been argued that the working class, steeped in bourgeois ideology, is not likely to develop its own independent class analysis that leads to revolutionary agency. There is, of course, a dialectic among spontaneity, leadership, and organization.

Engels identifies his understanding of the importance of human agency when he refers to the "growing perception" of the irrationality of capital and the need to transform "the modes of production and exchange themselves" (p. 72). Essentially, the argument is that human energies directed at contributing to a postcapitalist future should not be limited to abstract reasoning but should focus on collecting evidence and analyzing concrete, material conditions, what he calls "...the stubborn facts of the existing system of production" (p. 72). This is a conceptualization of dialectical change, marked by a dynamic interaction and antagonism between the parts and the whole. Making a larger point concerning the magnitude and mass of surplus-value, Marx (1867/1983) notes how Hegel discovered "that merely quantitative differences beyond a certain point pass into qualitative changes" (p. 309). As an example, Marx points to "the guilds of the Middle Ages" that "tried to prevent by force the transformation of the master of a trade into a capitalist by limiting the number of laborers that could be employed by one master" (p. 309). Engels highlights the process by which the bourgeoisie broke free from the feudal barriers to the unlimited accumulation of surplus labor-hours. In his discussion, he therefore identifies the bourgeoisie as the active, human agent of change ushering in the capitalistic era:

> The bourgeoisie broke up the feudal system and built upon its ruins the capitalist order of society, the kingdom of free competition, of personal liberty, of the equality before the law of all commodity owners, of all the rest of the capitalist blessings. (Engels, 1880/2007, p. 72)

As with the transition from feudalism to capitalism, there too will be active revolutionary agents of change with the transition out of capitalism. What is uncertain, however, is the nature of this movement. That is, will it be progressive or reactionary? Due to the long-term negative effects of cultural hegemony on labor, a postcapitalist future could very well be more authoritarian and fascist than the authoritarianism and fascism of today. Countering the current hegemony is therefore a pressing challenge for critical pedagogy. Regardless of the nature of its manifestation, Engels identifies this agent as primarily within those who rely on a wage to survive, the working class, which, from this Marxist conception of social class, is nearly all of humanity, from those whose lives are cut short from the extreme exploitation rampant in so-called third-world sweat shops to relatively privileged university professors in the so-called first world (despite the great diversity of privilege and suffering within labor). Making the point that social change tends to come from social classes that are experiencing unresolvable structural barriers to becoming and who are aware of their own material conditions, using capitalism as an example, Engels (1880/2007) is instructive:

> The new productive forces have already outgrown the capitalist mode of using them. And this conflict between productive forces and modes of production is not a conflict engendered in the mind of man, like that between original sin and divine justice. It exists in fact, objectively, outside us, independently of the will and actions of even the men who brought it on. Modern socialism is nothing but the reflex, in thought, of this conflict in fact; its ideal reflection in the minds, first, of the class directly suffering under it, the working class. (p. 73)

This too is where our critical pedagogy should look for a concrete understanding of the world that we confront. With this in mind, Marx's (1875/2002) critique and outline of the transition out of the capitalist mode of production remains highly relevant. The first step in this transition is to ensure that workers, after the aforementioned deductions for education and whatnot are made, gets back exactly what he or she puts in. According to Marx's labor theory of value, in the initial stages of developing a postcapitalist society, producers would not be cheated out of their surplus labor-hours. The worker gets back from society a voucher representing the amount of labor hours he puts in. Marx (1875/2002) therefore states that "the same amount of labor which he has given to society in one form, he receives back in another" (p. 8). While this formula for the exchange of equal values currently regulates the exchange of commodities (in theory at least) in its altered form, "no one can give anything except his labor, and because, on the other hand, nothing can pass into the ownership of individuals except individual means of consumption" (p. 9). As Marx (1885/1978) puts it in the second volume of *Capital*, "There is no reason why the producers should not receive paper tokens permitting them to withdraw an amount corresponding to their labour time from the social consumption stocks. But these tokens are not money; they do not circulate" (p. 434).

However, while this formulation is referred to as an advance, this advance is qualified as still being "stigmatized by a bourgeois limitation" (p. 9) encompassed within the notion of *rights*. Marx (1875/2002) explains that "the right of the producers is *proportional* to the labor they supply; the equality consists in the fact that measurement is made with an *equal standard*, labor" (ibid.). The limitation resides within the fact that there exist natural differences between individuals in terms of their capacity to labor—in terms of duration, skill, type, and intensity. Consequently, "this *equal* right is an unequal right for unequal labor" (ibid.). This is the limited nature of rights. Using an equal standard for unequal individuals can only serve to reinforce inequality. Using labor as a standard measure, for example, ignores everything else but labor. It ignores the long-lasting effects of racial, gender, and class discrimination that, if not concretely addressed, will persist. Some workers have children and are responsible for dependents and will receive less of the total social product, for example. While these limitations can be overcome, Marx argues they are unavoidable in the first stages of communist society.

> In a higher phase of communist society, after the enslaving subordination of individuals under division of labor, and therewith also the antithesis between mental and manual labor, has vanished; after labor, from a mere means of life, has itself become the prime necessity of life; after the productive forces have also increased with the all-around development of the individual, and all the springs of co-operative wealth flow more abundantly—only then can the narrow horizon of bourgeois right be fully left behind and society inscribe on its banners: from each according to his ability, to each according to his needs! (p. 10)

The focus on equalizing distribution and consumption is misplaced because these processes are mere "consequences of the distribution of the conditions of production themselves" (ibid.), which, once corrected, can lead to an altered distribution of the means of consumption.

Placing this analysis within our overarching argument in this book, what Marx is concretizing here in his outline of a postcapitalist society is his corrected version of Hegel's dialectic, or the theory of movement and change propelled by contradictions inherent within the *logic* of capital itself. Marx's conception of communism represents the positive that already exists as a structurally determined potentiality within the negative (i.e., bourgeois society). It is the internal contradictions within the negative that compel but does not predetermine it to change. The absolute idea is becoming. Hegel conceptualized this movement as the negation of the negation. We might say that one way to understand this double negativity is by the process of eliminating the external and internal barriers to becoming. We can see this in Marx's multiple stages of the development of capitalist society outlined above. Dunayevskaya's theory of state capitalism was informed by this analysis and reading of Marx's (1875/2002) *Critique of the Gotha Programme*. That is, she critiqued the Soviet Union for ending the struggle for communism after just the initial armed-struggle stage in the revolutionary process of becoming.

While the political critique wielded may have been missing historical and material elements, the theoretical point that we take from it is that a Marxist pedagogy of becoming begins exactly where we are. For us, it is selling our capacity to teach and produce research in a teacher education program at a unionized, state-owned, traditionally working-class university in West Chester, PA, USA, and in a teacher education program at a private university in Syracuse, NY, USA. This is precisely why we provided examples of the university and education context. Laborers selling their human commodity in other aspects of industry have their concrete conditions of production as their place of departure. Collectively, in all our diversity of skill, ability, and wage, all workers face a common antagonistic capitalist negative counterpart and a capitalist economy that has entered a permanent stage of descent and perpetual crisis that threatens all of humanity and the very system of nature itself. This pedagogy of becoming is not a casual call to action but comes with a sense of urgency that is not possible to exaggerate or overstate.

Consequently, we might say that this critical pedagogy of becoming is intended to represent a rebellion in education. That is, this critical pedagogy is informed by the same insights informing Marx's hypothetical wage workers, who uncover and become conscious of the fact that "wages are not what they *appear* to be, namely, the *value*, or *price*, *of labor*, but only a masked form for the *value*, or *price*, *of labor power*," and, as a result, develop a full understanding of capitalism and become socialist organizers. Put another way, we might say that the goal of a Marxist critical pedagogy is to facilitate a class and self-consciousness within students and teachers similar to that of the "...slaves who have at last got behind the secret of slavery and broken out in rebellion" (p. 15). As suggested above, this critical pedagogy is so out of fashion at the present moment in the larger mainstream critical pedagogy community at the center of the capitalist power base, the United States, that Marxist educators often relate to Marx's dismay of how many socialists adopted the limited analysis showcased within the Gotha Programme.

Contrary to the Gotha Programme, what Marx is laying out is a nuanced analysis of "what transformation will the state undergo in communist society" and what "social functions will remain in existence" that currently exist (p. 18). In regard to education, Marx critiques the Programme for advocating for universal education because it already existed as such in the U.S., Germany, Switzerland, and elsewhere during his time. Rather, the Gotha Programme should have advocated for technical education that is both theoretical and practical. This approach to education was designed to reunite mental and manual labor to overcome the estrangement of capitalist production. That is, the extreme division of labor in capitalism reduced some to thinking (i.e., engineering, management, etc.) and others to doing (manual labor, deprofessionalized teaching, etc.). In another statement, Marx advocates for "an early combination of productive labor with education," claiming such an agenda "is one of the most potent means for the transformation or present-day society" (p. 22). This is no simple vocational education, which is nothing more than a means of perpetuating the division of mental and manual labor. Marx, rather, is laying out how society might function with the abolition of the idle class, the bourgeoisie. What if everyone was expected to work and think as the foundation of a society based upon the ethic of *each according to his or her ability* and *each according to her or his need*? In short, Marx was against any external force or authority that operates behind the backs of producers. Consequently, Marx disagreed with the state on capitalism having any influence on education, plainly stating that "government and church should rather be equally excluded from any influence on the school" (p. 21). It is rather *the state* that needs to be educated by *the people* (i.e., the proletarians).

Communism and a Marxist Critical Pedagogy of Becoming

The purpose of this final section is to spell out more concretely what a Marxist critical pedagogy of becoming might look like by synthesizing, extending, and explicitly formulating the points made above.

First, the critical pedagogy we have constructed here begins with recognizing the deep-seated, religious-like anti communism that is propagated at nearly every turn in U.S. society. From schools to news outlets, from popular to alternative media, and from the extreme political right wing and the left wing, we are constantly told that communism equals totalitarianism and a life without color. As Jodi Dean (2012) has put it, we are currently limited by a teleological, historicist narrative of "The chain communism-Soviet Union-Stalinism-collapse" (p. 32). Our critical pedagogy begins with an outright rejection of not only this chain, however, but also, and more importantly, a rejection of the narrative upon which it rests. It begins, that is, with a dialectical and historical-materialist account of actually existing socialism of yesterday and today, with an understanding of the historical events and forces that shape(d) actual policies and practices. Such an objective appraisal avoids both uncritically glorifying and condemning socialist and workers' states—as well as their governing bodies. The communist struggle today does not seek, of course, to replicate the communism of yesterday but seeks to create a new socialism for the 21st century.

Second, our critical pedagogy is oriented toward the totality of life. What we mean by this is that it is not merely focused on developing critical consciousness and reclaiming time for creativity in education as ends in themselves but insofar as they contribute to the overall struggle of liberating nature and the social productive forces from private ownership. This, of course, entails—and is a necessary prerequisite for—the liberation of the individual subject. In stark contrast to mainstream, domesticated currents that put critical pedagogy forward as a method of teaching and learning, we insist that critical pedagogy is part of a movement toward the radical transformation of the totality of social relations, which entails the *abolition* of capitalism and private-property-based social relations. This means—and this point is absolutely crucial—that our critical pedagogy is interested in combating neoliberalism only because neoliberalism is the current configuration of capitalism and the capital relation today. We are not interested in fighting neoliberal privatizations in the name of a kinder, gentler capitalism (which is always only kinder and gentler for some, of course). Or, more strategically speaking, we are interested in fighting neoliberalism insofar as that fight allows us to lay bare the fundamental logic of capital upon which it rests.

Third, a critical pedagogy of becoming connects to and builds upon global struggles—successful and defeated—against exploitation and oppression. As such, we look to the struggles of teachers, students, and workers in Greece and Mexico and in Quebec and Turkey in solidarity. We seek to articulate their struggles in our own cities, workplaces, and schools. We identify as allies with the oppressed who are waging their struggle for liberation *through* and *with* the apparatus of the state, such as it is occurring in, for example, Cuba and Venezuela. We also connect our struggle at home with those peoples and nations under attack—or threat of attack—by U.S. imperialism. Ever since the dissolution and overthrow of the Soviet Union and the Eastern Bloc socialist countries, the globe has been the victim of an aggressive campaign to overthrow any government that has remained independent of or antagonistic to global capital and its imperialist hawks in NATO and the U.S. Pentagon. This was the logic behind the overt wars on Iraq, Afghanistan, and Libya, U.S. intervention in Ukraine, the partitioning of the Sudan, and the ongoing war on Syria; it is the logic behind the covert wars (by economic sanctions, drones, and other means) on Iran, the Democratic People's Republic of Korea, Venezuela, Cuba, Eritrea, and China.

When evaluating and, ultimately, judging struggles as they erupt across the globe, then, we must always inquire into the *class character* of these struggles and what effect these struggles will have in relation to the global totality that is dominated by imperialism. This is, again, why the framework of the global class war is so crucial. Further, we must ask ourselves what effect *our support* of those movements will likely have. The results of such analysis will not always make us popular, particularly given the velocity and impact of U.S. propaganda. Take, for example, the recent U.S. war on Libya in 2011. This war was portrayed by alternative and mainstream media as a popular, democratic uprising against a ruthless tyrant, and this narrative was embraced by many on the left. Yet in Libya, there was no mass movement, no working-class or peasant character evident; it was immediately an armed right-wing insurrection that began with the splintering of the government (see Forte, 2012). Actually, to be more precise, there was a mass movement, but it was in support of the government, or, rather, in defense of the nation from imperialism and its rebel allies. To oppose the rebels and support Libyan self-defense at this particular moment meant isolation from not only the liberals but also much of the left.

Fourth, the critical pedagogy intimated here must be based on critical, rigorous concepts and formulations. As Marx chastised Lassalle for his uncritical formulations such as the "proceeds of labor" or the "prevailing state of society," we must ensure that the frameworks within which we act are formulated at an appropriate level of abstraction (see Ollman, 1993). An example of an uncritical, inaccurately abstracted concept in many brands of critical pedagogy that we must subject to critique is that of "student." Critical pedagogues, so it goes, must be student centered, we must work to transform the lives of our students, and so on. The critical question we ask here is: which students? For "students" is in many ways a mystifying category, one that can serve to blur and even render invisible class lines. After all, the children of the bourgeoisie can sit in desks adjacent to the children of the working class, particularly in institutions of higher education. Thus, a critical pedagogy of becoming, based on a class analysis, is oriented toward *working-class and other oppressed students*, not students in general. Or perhaps we could say that critical pedagogy should work to transform the lives of all students, just in different ways: it should work to liberate oppressed students and repress students from the oppressing class (so that, in accordance with Freire, they can be humanized).

The fifth point is tied to and follows from the fourth: A critical pedagogy of becoming isn't just about transformation; it is about transformation toward communism. This is a radical and necessary departure from contemporary critical pedagogy (and left educational theory more generally) that is cloaked in talk of "democracy" and, more radically, "anticapitalism." The former signifier is particularly dangerous and reactionary today. As Dean (2012) states, "for leftists to refer to their goals as a struggle for democracy is strange. It is a defense of the status quo, a call for more of the same" (p. 57). Further, it "avoids the fundamental antagonism between the 1 percent and the rest of us by acting as if the only thing really missing was participation" (pp. 57–58). In other words, the extent to which critical pedagogy embraces calls for democracy is the extent to which it ignores and sublimates class struggle. Marx criticized the Lassallian call for a "free people's state" in the Gotha Programme on similar grounds. Marx insisted that the state was always occupied and wielded by a specific class for their self-interest. Calls for democracy obscure this reality and cover over the social relations of production under capitalism. As Lukàcs (1924/2009) writes, this move has the effect "*of disorganizing these classes as classes* and pulverizing them into atoms easily manipulated by the bourgeoisie" (p. 64), transforming "proletarians" into "citizens." While critical and other pedagogies based on anticapitalism represent an improvement on those emanating from vague conceptions of democracy, they nonetheless hesitate, remaining stuck in the moment of critique. They are fixated, in other words, on the process of "becoming" and are not concerned with what this becoming will become. While we do not claim to articulate the future in advance, we do insist, as Marx did in his critique, that we imagine this future and locate its potentialities within the subjective and objective tendencies present within capitalism today.

This leads us to our sixth and final point. This point is derived not so much from the *content* of Marx's critique but from its purpose and overall context: namely, the necessity for organization and the Party. The purpose of Marx's intervention, after all, was not based on a desire for some theoretical consistency or purity; on the contrary, it was motivated by a (well-founded) concern of what effects the theoretical formulations and concepts in the Programme would have on the workers' and socialist movements in Germany. Interestingly, Marx never wrote a book or pamphlet about the party-form, yet the necessity of the party was what underwrote his life's work. It is, after all, not merely the working class as such, but the organized working class that represents the ultimate threat to the rule of capital. The Party, in other words, is that which mediates *becoming*, defending it from capitalism and advancing it toward communism.

Notes

1. Moreover, *surplus* generally is an integral aspect of any society (to deal with means of production or subsistence that do not yield useful effects for a long time, to deal with natural disasters, etc.).
2. At the time of this writing, the occupation has ended but the movement continues. Check out http://www.thegeneralbody.org for updates.

· 4 ·

THE "CYNICAL RECKLESSNESS" OF CAPITAL: MACHINERY, BECOMING, AND REVOLUTIONARY MARXIST SOCIAL STUDIES EDUCATION

Introduction

In this chapter, we draw out an example of the process of becoming through negation by turning to the transition from industry to manufacture. We examine the birth of modern "education" as a result of this transition. The development of modern education is connected to contemporary right-wing education "reforms," and in this area, we pay particular attention to the form and content of such reforms, as well as their effect on labor-power. Then, in order to make our critical pedagogy of becoming even more concrete, we sketch what a Revolutionary Marxist Social Studies education might look like and how it can harness the negation of the negation to push forward the transition to communism.

In particular, we show how the emergence of the industrial era of capitalism developed out of the manufacturing era through the invention of machines that would radically displace human muscle power with non human power, such as coal, wind, and electricity. In other words, the manufacturing era would produce the machine that would then destroy the very manufacturing era to which it gave birth. This revolution in production would lead to a legislative mandate for compulsory education as a result of the machine displacing human power, making possible the employment of young children and the subsequent intellectual degradation of the child and society in general. In other words, the capitalist state attempted, however feebly, to legislatively intervene in order to save society from capital, which we take as a powerful challenge to the bourgeois assumption of the inherent benevolence of capital. With the further development of the means of production and the changing educational needs of capital, the educated worker would be born. With a Revolutionary Marxist Social Studies education, we believe that the educated worker could be poised to push the very system that created her toward a more democratic, socialist alternative. Of the many themes that run through the pages of Marx's *Capital,* the one highlighted here is the tendency of new developments, both qualitative and quantitative, to emerge out of old conditions.

We outline the ways in which the era of manufacture developed into the more technically complex industrial era through the advancement of machinery. What this discussion points to is how the internal logic of capital drives it toward more technically extensive instruments of production and these instruments of production are designed to lead to growing economic exploitation and intellectual alienation and degradation. We then argue that these tendencies paved the way for increasingly formalized and standardized forms of education. In the process, we argue that the role of education and the educator have a similar effect on the production of labor as the machine has on the production of products. Finally, we argue that because capital seems to be in a declining phase marked by escalating immiseration, the need for ideological control to counter the threat of working-class rebellion is also rising. It is within this context that No Child Left Behind and now Race to the Top and the Common Core State Standards can be best understood. Focusing specifically on social studies, we argue that with the assistance of Marx, the educated worker can play a more decisive role in creating a communist alternative out of today's system of global capitalism. This is the foundation of a Revolutionary Marxist Social Studies.

The Creative Economy Fetish

Recently, many educational and other theorists have been interested in the potential opened up with the transformation from the industrial economy to the "creative" or "cognitive" economy. This view holds that advanced capitalist economies like the U.S. have transitioned from producing "hard" commodities toward cognitive and cultural commodities, like information, communications, and languages. Or, perhaps more accurately, the creative economy is less concerned with the physicality of the commodity than with "the informational and cultural content of the commodity" (Lazzarato, 1996, p. 133). The physicality of the commodity is, in this schema, subordinated to its creative content. The commodity produced is reflective of changes in productive relations. The move toward the creative economy, then, is located with the crisis of capitalism in the late 1970s to the early 1980s, with the breakdown of Fordist production arrangements and the increasing and globalizing flexibility of capital and labor relations. There are numerous (and conflicting) theories about the rise of the creative economy, but they generally refer to the increasing role of information, knowledge, and communication in the production process.

Marxist readings of the creative economy locate its transition within industrialism and tend to focus on a few pages from Marx's *Grundrisse* notebooks referred to as the "fragment on machines." Marx is here writing about the rise of machinery in capitalism and is anticipating future developments. He writes that:

> The accumulation of knowledge and of skill, of the general productive forces of the social brain, is thus absorbed into capital, as opposed to labour, and hence appears as an attribute of capital, and more specifically of *fixed capital*, in so far as it enters into the production process as a means of production proper. (Marx, 1939/1973, p. 694)

Some Marxists, particularly from the autonomist tradition, argue that Marx is anticipating the turn toward the creative economy in that he emphasizes the increasing importance of knowledge, skill, and intellect in the production process. Further, Marx refers to the "social brain" or "general intellect" as a product of capitalist development. The general intellect signals the ways in which knowledge becomes generated *throughout* society, so that it is no longer only produced in the halls of academia or the labs of medical corporations. Indeed, it is hard to imagine language being produced in isolation or behind the walls of a factory.

While there is much value in the changing role of information, knowledge, and communication in capitalist production processes, some proponents of the creative economy thesis end up viewing this as a homogenous process, thereby ignoring the radical class differences within any such economy. While we concede that the role of information is increasingly important in capitalist value production, as demonstrated in the transition from manufacture proper to the industrial era of the machine highlighted throughout this essay, it is not determinant or even hegemonic. Further, as educationalists, we believe it is crucial to point out how only some sectors of society are privileged to participate in the creative economy, at least formally. Again, something like language *is* produced throughout society, not only in universities but also, for example, in ghettos, through graffiti art, hip-hop, and everyday conversation. Yet it is only when capitalism expropriates and incorporates this into production that it becomes commodified and enters into circuits of exchange and valorization.

Further, cognitive capitalism ignores the often mind-numbing work that so many are forced to perform. This is not limited to the service economy, either. Even teachers, under the Common Core Standards movement, are increasingly alienated from their own intellect. Thus, while capitalist production has become increasingly dependent upon the generation of information and knowledge, this has not resulted in a general increase in the intellect of individual workers. In fact, we argue that the opposite has been the case and that today creativity and intellect are cultivated in slim sectors of society, while the majority are discouraged and disallowed from developing skills such as creative or critical thinking.

From Manufacture to Machinery

We begin with the notion that perpetual economic growth, which has always included a cognitive component, combined with the insight that only human labor has the capacity to augment new value, results in a tendency toward the degradation and deadly abuse of the laborer. Describing the advent of the manufacturing period of capital's development, Marx (1867/1983) writes:

> An increased number of laborers under the control of one capitalist is the natural starting point, as well of co-operation generally…Hence, it is a law, based on the very nature of manufacture, that the minimum amount of capital, which is bound to be in the hands of each capitalist, must keep increasing; in other words, the transformation into capital of the social means of production and subsistence must keep extending. (pp. 359–360)

Under capitalist development, humanity in general—save a small minority of capitalists and landlords—becomes collectively organized and externally commanded, increasing the efficiency and productivity of society's productive force. As a result, the will and intellect of each of the separate parts are suppressed:

> Manufacture proper not only subjects the previously independent workman to the discipline and command of capital, but, in addition, creates a hierarchic gradation of the workmen themselves...It converts the laborer into a crippled monstrosity, by forcing his detail dexterity at the expense of a world of productive capabilities and instincts...Not only is the detail work distributed to the different individuals, but the individual himself is made the automatic motor of a fractional operation...which makes man a mere fragment of his own body. (p. 360)

The dehumanization and exploitation of the laborer, that is, is not driven by bad people (i.e., greedy capitalists) but rather by capital's own internal logic. The contemporary creative turn, in this context, represents not a new era but an intensification of the tendency toward the intellectual and material degradation of the laborer. The division of labor represented by the creative laborers has only further divorced intellectual labor from manual labor, highlighted by the overwhelming dominance of high takes testing that tend to function at a very low cognitive level. Creative laborers such as engineers design computer machines, for example, that further reduce already mangled workers into even more degraded and dehumanized appendages. The problem of contemporary immiseration (Hill, 2013) is not that capitalism is not properly regulated but that when done correctly, the result is the intellectual degradation and premature exhaustion and death of the laborer—one of capital's primary contradictions. Not only is the outcome of unfettered capitalism the tendency to work laborers to death, but even highly regulated capital tends toward the intellectual degradation and permanent and extending alienation of the producers. This tendency is an outcome of the organizational development of capital itself:

> The knowledge, the judgment, and the will, which, though in ever so small a degree, are practiced by the independent peasant or handicraftsman...these faculties are now required only for the workshop as a whole. Intelligence in production expands in one direction, because it vanishes in many others. What is lost in the detail laborers, is concentrated in the capital that employs them...This separation begins in simple co-operation, where the capitalist represents to the single workman, the oneness and the will of the associated labor...It is completed in modern industry, which makes

science a productive force distinct from labor and presses it into the service of capital. (p. 361)

Marx refers to this concentration of what is essentially *creative capital* as a result of "industrial pathology," wherein workers are degraded and all of humanity's cultural achievements and civilizations are violently ground and bleached out of the fabric that binds humans together. As the means of production develops and advances, the intellectual level of society declines. Marx cites Adam Smith on the stupidification of laborers as a product of the extreme division of labor. Smith argues that the state should provide laborers with a formal education as a solution to this phenomenon. However, Smith's French translator opposes, "education for the masses," not for reasons of prejudice or bias, but rather, for violating "the first law of the division of labor" (p. 362) (i.e., the separation between manual and mental labor). This reinforces his position that the harshness of capital is not motivated, initially, by the personality or biases of the capitalist, "for in money matters sentiment is out of place" (p. 234). The argument against educating the masses is therefore that it could possibly subvert the natural development of the division of labor because it violates the laws of capitalist accumulation, which require a single mind and vision directing the centrally organized masses of laborers working in concert through the direction of the machine. Marx is absolutely clear, however, that this separation of mental labor from manual labor results in the execution of the human being and tends toward the draining of society's collective potentiality. Again, this result was not necessarily motivated by a hatred of the laborer but by the quest to most efficiently augment value. The hatred and cultural devaluing of the laborer are rather an afterthought, an ideological necessity of a system indifferent to matters outside of expanding the universal equivalent. Making this point, Marx elaborates:

> …Manufacture is but one particular method of begetting relative surplus-value, or of augmenting at the expense of the laborer the self-expansion of capital…It increases the social productive power of labor, not only for the benefit of the capitalist instead of for that of the laborer, but it does this by crippling the individual laborers. It creates new conditions for the lordship of capital over labor. (p. 364)

While the productivity of labor and the subsequent increase in the proportion of surplus labor as compared to necessary labor is greatly enhanced during this period, "many obstacles" remain, prohibiting "the full development of the peculiar tendencies of manufacture" (p. 367). Marx points specifically to the "insubordination of the workmen" whose handicraft skills, however fragmented and degraded, remained the "foundation of manufacture" (ibid.). Eventually, the barrier posed by what workers still held in their possession—their physical strength, human power, and intellect—was subverted by the invention of the machine. This shift, of course, was gradual but decisive:

> At a given stage in its development, the narrow technical basis on which manufacture rested, came into conflict with requirements of production that were created by manufacture itself. One of its most finished creations was the workshop for the production of the instruments of labor themselves, including especially the complicated mechanical apparatus then already employed...This workshop, the product of the division of labor in manufacture, produced in its turn—machines. It is they who swept away the handicraftsman's work as the regulating principle of social production. (p. 368)

Machinery subjects the laborer to it, degrading and dominating the individual worker. Once machine power replaces human power, the influence of the laborer in resisting the encroachment of capital is severely limited, and a new era of capitalism is ushered in. That is, what the laborers still partially held in their possession as a bargaining chip for slowing down their own exploitation and premature exhaustion was the specified knowledge needed to command their tools. With the machine factory, that knowledge is rendered redundant. Similarly, standardized, premade exams and curricula, as argued above, work to alienate educators from their specialized knowledges, reducing them to minders of the education machine and subsequently limiting their collective leverage. Marx describes the manifestation of this system with vivid imagery:

> An organized system of machines, to which motion is communicated by the transmitting mechanism from a central automaton, is the most developed form of production by machinery. Here we have, in the place of the isolated machine, a mechanical monster whose body fills whole factories, and whose demon power, at first veiled under the slow and measured motions of his giant limbs, at length breaks out into the fast and furious whirl of his countless working organs. (p. 382)

True to his dialectical conception of change that we outlined in Chapter 1, Marx captures the way in which the era of manufacture embodied its own negation as the industrial period developed from within its own tendencies. This is another example of quantitative shifts, having reached a certain point, becoming qualitative transformations. Consequently, when the production of machines eventually replaces human labor-power, a qualitative change in the forces of production takes place. From here, Marx explores the effect of machines producing machines on the value they transfer to the products they produce.

Marx acknowledges that on the surface, it is evident that "by incorporating both stupendous physical forces, and the natural sciences, with the process of production, Modern Industry raises the productiveness of labor to an extraordinary degree" (p. 387). However, like other aspects of constant capital, machinery "creates no new value, but yields up its own value to the product it serves to beget," and modern machinery "is loaded with value" (p. 387). Like the human laborer in manufacture whose subjectivity is consumed through the production process, the machine too transfers its own value (i.e., the raw material or constant capital and human labor or variable capital employed for its production) into the material that becomes a product. Marx goes to great lengths to demonstrate that the slow rate of wear and tear and the extreme efficiency of some means that the value they transmit through production can become so insignificant that they can appear to "do their work gratuitously, just like the forces furnished by nature without the help of man" (p. 388). Consequently, "the productiveness of a machine is…measured by the human labor-power it replaces" (p. 391). In other words, machine power is preferred to human power if the amount of labor required for its production is less than the amount of labor it displaces. This is desirable for the *individual* capitalist, in that it allows him to capture relative surplus-value. Yet it is detrimental to capitalism as a whole, because the system lives by exploiting human labor-power. Because the machine was so successful at replacing the physical strength of the laborer at an extraordinary rate, the capitalist was no longer limited to the grown man for labor but could now throw his entire family upon the labor market, thereby further devaluing labor and thus increasing, astronomically, the accumulation of surplus labor-hours.

Capitalism and the Birth of Compulsory "Education"

The value of labor-power was no longer determined by the number of hours required to reproduce the existence of a single laborer but rather those required to reproduce the existence of the laborer and his whole family. Even wages may, as a result, have been raised; the capitalist was now able to accumulate the surplus labor of the worker's wife and children. Consequently, "machinery, while augmenting the human material that forms the principal object of capital's exploiting power, at the same time raises the degree of exploitation" (p. 395). Ultimately, this transformation revolutionizes the relationship between the worker and the capitalist: "previously, the workman sold his own labor-power, which he disposed of nominally as a free agent. Now he sells wife and child. He has become a slave dealer" (p. 396).

The result of this transformation was a quite horrible condition in which children who appeared to be 13 years of age, determined by a physician employed by the industrialists seeking to swell their ranks of laborers, toiled in factories. Children too small to labor were often neglected and malnourished or poisoned with opiates, as their caretakers were compelled to expend their own labor capacity in the factories or some other branch of production where the cost of their labor was less than an animal or a machine. While the physical exhaustion and death of women and children led to the depletion of many English towns, Marx (1867/1983) also comments at length on the intellectual degradation of children, which led the English Parliament to "make elementary education a compulsory condition to the 'productive' employment of children under 14 years, in every industry subject to the Factory Acts" (p. 400).

Predictably enough, because the industrialist—at this point in capital's historical development—saw no advantage of having a properly educated workforce, what passed as education was little more than the stockpiling of children into a room for a required duration of time. Of course, this "education" did nothing to reverse "the intellectual desolation artificially produced by converting immature human beings into mere machines for the fabrication of surplus-value" (p. 399). The education of laborers would not be taken seriously by capitalist employers until they were convinced that schooling was a necessary cost of production and reproduction, both materially and ideologically.

Contributing to the need for ideological indoctrination is the contradictory effect of machines under the logic of capital. While machines increase the productivity of labor, they simultaneously reduce the amount of variable capital required for production. Because machines, as constant capital, produce no new value, the overall absolute surplus-value declines, leading to struggles over the lengthening of the workday. Marx concludes that "machinery sweeps away every moral and natural restriction on the length of the working day" (p. 408). Paradoxically, then, "the most powerful instrument for shortening labor-time, becomes the most unfailing means for placing every moment of the laborer's time and that of his family, at the disposal of the capitalist for the purpose of expanding the value of his capital" (ibid.). Working-class resistance eventually led to legal restraints on the length of the working day. Just as soon as such limits were imposed, capitalists began to increase the intensification of the working day through speeding up the machines and paying stricter attention to the efficiency of operations. This way, capital did not lose profits as a result of shortening the working day. However, what was sacrificed with intensification was "the health of the workman" and "his capacity to work" since intensification consists of a "closer filling up of the pores of the working-day" and "squeezing out more labor in a given time" (pp. 410–417).

Intensification breeds working-class resistance, requiring capital to employ more effective forms of ideological indoctrination; it is precisely this need that formal education served. This points to another paradox: as the machine makes redundant the skilled worker and thus eliminates the need for formal education, the emergence of the unskilled worker increases immiseration and thus working-class resistance, which in turn increases the need for the ideological management most efficiently and consistently offered by formal education. This paradox helps us understand education policy in the contemporary context that seems to sacrifice intelligence for obedience. The exception is elite education, which emphasizes intelligence and problem-solving skills at the expense of obedience and passivity found in more working-class forms of schooling. The overwhelming vast majority of us experience education as an exaggerated series of rituals consisting of exercises in following directions and obedience training at the great expense of critical thinking and creativity.

Industrial capitalism demands absolute subordination of the laborer's will to "the central driving power" of capital to achieve maximum efficiency and thus productivity (p. 419). Unlike the use of machines in precapitalist production in which labor controlled the "mechanical automaton," only in capitalism are both the unconscious machine and the conscious laborer reduced to subordinated automatons. Consequently, the laborer's intellectual potential and quality of life are negatively affected. Laborers on both sides of the Atlantic certainly complained of the alienating and intellectually degrading tendency of the shift from manufacture to modern industrialism during the mid-19th century. For example, in 1899, representatives of the Boot and Shoe Workers' Union reported to the U.S. Congress on the intellectual and economic degradation brought on by the advent of the machine factory. As the perspective of labor is indispensable here, a sizable excerpt is provided:

Eleven years ago I used to be able to earn myself, lasting shoes, from $18 to $35 a week, according to how hard I wanted to work. Today, on the same class of work, I would not be able, on any job in the city, to make more than $15 or $12…The manufacturers equip themselves to turn out their product in a shorter time…He becomes a machine…One [might] wonder how a man could pick up and lay down 4,800 shoes in a day, to say nothing of putting them on a jack into a machine and having them nailed on…In these old shops, years ago, one man owned the shop; he took in…3, 4, 5, or 6 others, neighbors, came in there and sat down and made shoes right in their laps, and there was no machinery. Everybody was at liberty to talk; they were all politicians…Of course, under these conditions, there was absolute freedom and exchange of ideas, they naturally would become more intelligent than shoe workers can at the present time, when they were driving each man to see how many shoes he can handle, and when he is surrounded by noisy machinery. And another thing, this nervous strain on a man doing just one thing over and over again, must necessarily have a wearing effect on him; and his ideals, I believe, must be lowered. (Meltzer, 1967, pp. 8–10)

The immiseration (Hill, 2013) unique to capitalist development stems not only from the degradation of the laborer's physical strength and objective being but also from the degradation of her mental powers, atrophied by an *enforced* lack of use. Immiseration is both physical and mental (Malott, Hill, & Banfield, 2013). The tendency described so brutally in the above passage is inherent to capitalist development and has only continued to escalate into the present moment.

Again, this escalation characteristic of capital in general and the industrial era in particular developed out of the rise of the machine. This is one more example of old conditions giving way to new developments. Early on in *Capital,* Marx writes how the advanced division of labor characteristic of late feudalism implies the transformation of the producers' product into commodities and is therefore endowed with both an exchange-value and a use-value. As the master craftsmen and merchants developed into capitalists, the number of laborers they employed increased to the point where they no longer needed to contribute their own labor to the production process.

The immediate means of production in early capitalism were identical to that of feudalism. Through the era of manufacture, the tool was the primary instrument of production. Marx argues that one of the defining characteristics of a tool is that it is powered by human muscle and requires the laborer's knowledge and skill to operate. In this context, the laborer's labor-power is not merely physical strength but includes the intellectual skill required to know the technicalities of a trade. With human muscle, machines also replaced the laborer's intellect, as argued above:

> Along with the tool, the skill of the workman in handling it passes over to the machine. The capabilities of the tool are emancipated from the restraints that are inseparable from human labor-power. Thereby the technical foundation on which is based the division of labor in manufacture, is swept away. Hence, in the place of the hierarchy of specialized workmen that characterizes manufacture, there steps, in automatic factory, a tendency to equalize and reduce to one and the same level every kind of work that has to be done by the minders of the machines; in the place of artificially produced differentiations of the detail workmen, step the natural differences of age and sex. (p. 420)

As capitalism developed out of feudalism, there was a simultaneous increase in the rate of exploitation and alienation. Initially, it is the product of her labor from which the worker is alienated. Slowly, through the periods of manufacture and industry, the laborer increasingly becomes alienated from her own mental abilities and from what it means to be a natural being, consciously engaged and connected to the production of the system of nature. However, just because the machine factory swept away the division of labor theoretically, in practice "it hangs on...as a traditional habit handed down from manufacture, and is afterwards systematically re-molded and established in a more hideous form by capital, as a means of exploiting labor-power" (p. 422). Even though the laborer can move between machines with relative ease, she is instead shackled to a single machine, following its command. From childhood the laborer is fitted to and made an appendage of a machine. Everything from the spatiality and temporality of existence is subjected to the logic of the machine: "The worker's activity, reduced to a mere abstraction of activity, is determined on all sides by the movement of the machinery, and not the opposite" (Marx, 1939/1973, p. 693).

Not only is the cost of reproducing the worker's existence lowered (in the case of those commodities that are included in the determined value of labor-power), but "his helpless dependence upon the factory as a whole, and upon the capitalist, is rendered complete" (Marx, 1867/1983, p. 422). The alienation of humanity is also more complete, but, significantly, human agency and the potential for resistance can never be completely subverted—the potential for revolutionary transformation is thus forever present. Making explicit this state of alienation, Marx (1867/1983) explains:

At the same time the factory work exhausts the nervous system to the uttermost, it does away with the many-sided play of the muscles, and confiscates every atom of freedom, both in bodily and intellectual activity. The lightening of the labor, even, becomes a sort of torture, since the machine does not free the laborer from work, but deprives the work of all interest. Every kind of capitalist production, in so far as it is not only a labor-process, but also a process of creating surplus value, has this in common, that it is not the workman that employs the instruments of labor, but the instruments of labor that employ the workman...By means of its conversion into an automaton, the instrument of labor confronts the laborer, during the labor process, in the shape of capital, of dead labor, that dominates, and pumps dry, living labor power. The separation of the intellectual powers of production from the manual labor, and the conversion of those powers into the might of capital over labor, is, as we have already shown, finally completed by modern industry erected on the foundation of machinery. (p. 423)

It is within this context that industrialists very slowly began to view formal education as a necessary cost of production. The U.S. was one of the first countries to adopt such an approach to mass schooling, or common schooling. Horace Mann, the famous crusader for common schooling, went to great lengths to convince industrialists of the benefits of the educated worker as compared to the uneducated one. Mass education provided the vehicle for molding the mass of society's minds to accept the drudgery of work as inevitable and, paradoxically, honorable (i.e., the Protestant work ethic). Beginning in childhood, through schooling, youth could be socialized into a system of rigid codes of conduct, strict timetables, and obedience to authority in an effort to subvert the growing possibility of working-class uprisings. This need for obedience is made all the more apparent when we consider that the machine not only replaces human laborers and degrades the intellectual development of society in general but that "it is the most powerful weapon for repressing strikes" and that machines are "used as weapons against the revolts of the working-class" (pp. 435–436). This takes place not only through the eventual threat of redundancy but by consuming ever larger amounts of labor-power. That is, rather than just throwing workers onto the street, machines can have the effect of speeding up the expansion and deepening of production in general:

...In spite of the mass of hands actually displaced and virtually replaced by machinery, we can understand how the factory operatives, through the building of more mills and the extension of old ones in a given industry, may become more numerous than the manufacturing workmen and handicraftsmen that have been displaced. (p. 449)

What is revealed here is that machinery—potentially capable of reducing the length of the working day under socialism—under capitalism dramatically intensifies exploitation. This heightened exploitation of the laborers at a certain point in the development of machinery leads capitalists to attempt to reduce wages below what is socially necessary, which is a central feature of neoliberalism.

It is the dramatic intensification in the competition between capitalists that fuels this tendency. As machinery overtakes the whole of production, from the mining of coal and minerals to transport and communication, the "mode of production acquires an elasticity, a capacity for sudden extension by leaps and bounds that finds no hindrance except in the supply of raw material and in the disposal of the produce" (pp. 450–451). These labor-displacing, semi-automated developments in production provide the "weapons for conquering foreign markets" (p. 451), reducing the colonies to suppliers of raw materials and variable capital. Today, machinery, such as robotics and the Internet, has allowed sizable portions of production to be transferred from imperialist countries to the periphery and semiperiphery.

Educational Labor

The nightmare described by Marx since the 19th century has not receded but has escalated. This descending phase was mediated and to some degree stalled within advanced capitalist countries during the period of global revolution that we spoke about in Chapter 2. This was accomplished through force of law, widespread unionization, and increasingly on the backs of laborers in the so-called Third World through military intervention. It also arose as a direct response to victorious working-class and national liberation movements across the globe, which strengthened the global working-class movement in capitalist countries as well. This began to change in the late 1970s, when capitalism waged an internal and external counteroffensive against the proletarian class camp. To give a contemporary educational example of the tendency toward domination inherent in capital's use of the machine, we can look at the phenomena of online education and machine-like standardized exams and curricula that rob the teachers' labor of autonomy, freedom of movement, and critical abilities. Still, pockets of resistance and subversion decorate the global educational landscape like flowers sprouting from the structural cracks of a rigid and uncompromising artificial asphalt surface.

From the mid-19ᵗʰ century in the U.S., compulsory education was embraced as a form of social control. Bowles and Gintis (1976) argue convincingly that the evidence for this purpose of early common schooling, in part, can be found in the fact that while 75% of the workforce were literate, only 20% of jobs required that skill. Consequently, literacy was a somewhat unavoidable consequence of using education to shape the minds of laborers so they can understand their own interests and those of the capitalists as one and the same. The role of the educator, in adding value to the future useful worker through the process of schooling, includes not only providing the pupil with the skills required by capital—of which automation reduces the general level—but also with the worldview and ideology conducive to the interests of capital. It should be noted that while teachers and educators alike are part of the army of laborers because they must sell their human commodity for a wage to live, to access the products of other laborers' labor, the productiveness of their labor is a matter of somewhat complexity. In chapter 16 of the first volume of *Capital*, Marx (1867/1983) argues:

> If we may take an example from outside the sphere of production of material objects, a schoolmaster is a productive laborer, when, in addition to belaboring the heads of his scholars, he works like a horse to enrich the school proprietor. That the latter has laid out his capital in a teaching factory, instead of in a sausage factory, does not alter the relation. Hence the notion of a productive laborer implies not merely a relation between work and useful effect, between labor and product of labor, but also a specific, social relation of production, a relation that has sprung up historically and stamps the laborer as the direct means of creating surplus-value. To be a productive laborer is, therefore, not a piece of luck, but a misfortune. (p. 509)

While Marx's analysis here is helpful for understanding the relationship between educators and their various types of employers, as we argue below, education capitalists are driven by the value they can appropriate from education tax dollars and therefore do not actually augment new value. But the labor/capital relationship between the educator and management exists regardless of whether the educational capitalist augments new value or appropriates already produced value. This debate among Marxist educational theorists is not new.

For example, it has been noted that, traditionally, the labor of teachers creates no new value directly. That is, the teachers' wages, in this context, are appropriated from the total social product through a system of taxation and therefore represent the consumption of already produced value. Even in private schools where teachers' wages come from tuition and donations, the teacher does not confront management as a capitalist but as a regulator of the educational process and also represents the consumption of already produced value. More recently, however, for-profit management companies have worked successfully to change education policy, enabling them to privatize public schools, and, in the process, the state and federal education monies they receive. It has been argued that in this context the labor of teachers is directly profitable since their labor is purchased by the educational management company using the designated educational tax dollars with the intent of having some left over at the end of the labor (i.e., educational) process.

However, does the educator really create new value in the capitalistic sense? It might be argued that even in the case of the for-profit educational management companies, the labor of educators creates no new value but continues to represent the consumption of already produced value, a portion of which is accumulated by the management firm. What is more, the firm is driven by the same capitalistic impulse to accumulate as much value as possible as any other capitalist.

In regard to the effect of the teacher on the student, it might be compared to the way Marx describes the effect of the machine on the product it produces. The machine creates no new value but rather transfers the value of itself into the product it produces. The more value deposited into the machine, the more value it proportionally imparts to the product it produces. Likewise, the teacher, rather than producing new value, imparts its own value—regulated by a tightly controlled system of standards and competencies—into the students she educates. In this way, the teacher produces a regularity of the types and forms of living labor-power required by capital. The more educated the worker is, the more value it has absorbed—provided the education is deemed useful to capital—and thus the more valuable its labor-power. However, because capital is always driven to reduce the value of labor-power, educational costs are increasingly externalized to the workers themselves. The history of the labor movement has largely been the history of the struggle to increase the value of labor-power by claiming a great share of the value produced during the production process. The global movement of capital, often facilitated by military interventions, represents the quest to push down the value of labor-power. This push and pull represent the historic antagonism inherent within the labor/capital relationship.

It's also important to note that Marx's notion of productive versus unproductive labor has a strategic implication. Marx wrote *Capital*, after all, as a weapon for working-class struggle. By homing in on labor-power that directly produced surplus-value, Marx was pointing to a potentially weak link in the capitalist chain. Since Marx's time, however, education has become thoroughly generalized throughout capitalist countries. Thus, we argue that we must see educational labor—even though it is technically "unproductive"—as a crucial component in the reproduction of capitalist social relations. Educators can always subvert the use to which their labor is put. When this happens, those involved in the education process intentionally produce subjectivities antagonistic to capital. That is, the goal of a Marxist pedagogy is to produce a movement whose collective education is useful to anticapitalist revolution. Of course, this purpose of education is limited by the fact that we live in a world in which the system of nature is controlled by a minority of the population, the capitalists, and the state, part of the machinery of capital, and to live, one must possess a commodity (i.e., labor-power) that is useful to the capitalist (unless one has access to a sizable portion of already produced value they can live off of and thus not work). Critical educators must work to produce workers useful to capital but endowed with a critical consciousness dedicated to either making capital more equal or collectively pushing their own useful labor-power against the domination of capital. This latter model of change is based upon Marx's Hegelian conception of historical development, where the future always develops out of existing conditions.

Advancing a Revolutionary Marxist Pedagogy

Going back to our historical discussion, as production continued to develop in scope and complexity, the educational attainment required by capital steadily increased. The industrial era of capital ushered in the educated workforce, and with it, a new revolutionary potential and challenge to the intellectual degradation of previous eras of capitalist development. However, as Allman, McLaren, and Rikowski (2005) have noted, Marx pointed out that it is not only education that socially reproduces labor-power; the act of working itself serves the function of social reproduction, for "the labor process itself is a force that develops labor-power" (p. 150). While this point is extremely important for considering the pedagogical role of the act of selling one's labor commodity on the market for a wage, Marx (1867/1983) offers a more historical-developmentalist insight that contributes to the theme pursued throughout this chapter. That is, Marx points out how the developmental level of labor-power as it currently exists is not only the result of capitalist schooling and the labor process of capitalist production but the accumulated effect of the production of humanity:

> At the dawn of civilization the productiveness acquired by labor is small, but so too are the wants which develop with and by the means of satisfying them. Further, at that early period, the portion of society that lives on the labor of others is infinitely small compared with the mass of direct producers. Along with the progress in the productiveness of labor, that small portion of society increases both absolutely and relatively. Besides, capital with its accompanying relations springs up from an economic soil that is the product of a long process of development. The productiveness of labor that serves as its foundation and starting-point, is a gift, not of nature, but of a history embracing thousands of centuries. (p. 512)

What stands out here in our discussion of the cynical recklessness of capital is that the labor-power exploited by capital, in a sense, is the accumulated knowledge and experience produced through hundreds of thousands of years. However, the point of this chapter is not necessarily to outline the history of how human labor developed through time or of capital's changing needs in terms of the training and education required for the further development and production of useful labor. Rather, the objective here is to note that the future always exists as a potential immanent in the present. We might observe that as capital's development leads to increasingly educated laborers, at a certain point, the educated worker's quantitative transformation in terms of education eventually presents itself as a possibility that could give way to a qualitative transformation, despite the domesticating purpose of capitalist working-class education. While growing immiseration might increase the likelihood of laborers developing a critical analysis of capital and their role as variable capital, it is foolish to think that a particular experience will elicit a predetermined response or understanding. In other words, the growing educational attainment of laborers that has created—and sometimes realized—a potentially revolutionary response does not imply a form of essentialism or reductionism. Because the dominant ideology of society tends to be the ideology of the ruling power, the proletarian response to growing levels of educational attainment is far more likely to be interpreted as the realization of capital's promise of freedom and equality and not as a response to capital's changing labor needs and new forms of domination and exploitation.

What a critical pedagogy of becoming seeks to help students uncover is, in part, the logic of capital, driven by the quest to accumulate ever larger sums of surplus-value and thus to forever decrease the amount of the working day dedicated to the reproduction of the laborer through increasing productivity. Throughout the first volume of *Capital*, Marx takes great pains to highlight capital's deadliness, which always appears most explicitly when capital goes unregulated. For this reason, Marx often compares this omnipresent drive innate to the capitalist mode of production to the mythical werewolf whose terror will always emerge given the correct conditions (i.e., the absence of regulation and intervention). Today, we see this drive manifesting itself throughout much of the world, especially in so-called free-trade zones: in South America, the Caribbean, Eastern Europe, and elsewhere. Regarding the aftermath of legal regulations on the working day, Marx provides an example of just this tendency:

> The manufacturers had no need any longer to restrain themselves. They broke out in open revolt not only against the Ten Hours' Act, but against the whole legislation that since 1833 had aimed at restricting in some measure the "free" exploitation of labor-power. It was a pro-slavery rebellion in miniature, carried on for over two years with a cynical recklessness, a terrorist energy all the cheaper because the rebel capitalist risked nothing except the skin of his "hands." (p. 286).

Again, eventually in England, the Factory Acts of the 1860s—which Marx argued were "a necessary product of modern industry" (p. 480)—made compulsory elementary education mandatory for working youth. Marx noted the positive result on the child laborers who attended school. For these children, work and schooling each provided a break from the other, which had a positive impact on student-workers. As evidence, Marx points to reports by education inspectors who noted that children workers who only went to school half the day as compared to nonworking pupils who went to school the whole day "learnt quite as much and often more" (p. 483). So impressed was Marx with these educational developments that he came to some surprising conclusions concerning the future of education:

> The germ of the education of the future, an education that will, in the case of every child over a given age, combine productive labor with instruction and gymnastics, not only as one of the methods of adding to the efficiency of production, but as the only method of producing fully developed human beings. (p. 484)

The objective of Marx's pedagogy here is a poly-technical education focused on reuniting mental labor and manual labor with the arts and sports. This conception is no mere vocational education. However, before this or any socialist pedagogy can be implemented, we must successfully implement an anticapitalist pedagogy. That is, in the area of immediate production, we must first ensure that the laborer receives the full value of her expended labor-power and not just the portion that is necessary. A polytechnical education, in this context, is set against capital, uniting the theory of revolution with the practice of revolution aimed at realizing the communist potential that already exists within the current period of capitalist development. The highly deteriorated global capitalist economy, bursting with contradictions, is ripe for transformation.

Revolutionary Marxist Social Studies

As demonstrated above, machinery works to separate manual labor from the mental or intellectual aspect of production. Again, state and federal standards and high-stakes standardized exams function as a sort of industrial machine, displacing a certain amount of teachers' manual and mental labor. The teacher here becomes more and more of an automaton controlled by the curriculum and the process of schooling rather than an educator creating and directing instruction. Capital's utilization of robotics and computerization has contributed significantly to this tendency, reducing the teacher to an increasingly deskilled or unskilled appendage of the schooling machine. As immiseration escalates and the unresolvable antagonism between labor and capital becomes more apparent, there seems to be a corresponding tightening up and intensification of ideological control. Global capitalist education reform, and the U.S. in particular, has been moving toward policies that "restrict critical analysis of historical and contemporary events" (Westheimer, 2014, p. 130), with a renewed emphasis on flag education and authoritarian forms of patriotism. While U.S. state social studies standards have stressed the importance of multiple perspectives, such as comparative economics, there has more recently been an emphasis, coming from right-wing activism at the state level, on uncritically teaching "the importance of free enterprise in the U.S." (p. 131). What legitimate social studies remains will most likely continue to be based on the rote memorization of predetermined facts and narratives constructed from a traditional point of view (Jorgensen, 2014), that is, written from the perspective of the capitalist class. Similarly, Ross, Mathison, and Vinson (2014) conclude that:

> The Common Core State Standards are the most recent incarnation of curriculum documents that define what will be taught and how it will be taught in schools...

with an emphasis on "world-class" standards, 21ˢᵗ-century skills, and a logic that sees schools as serving the needs of corporate capitalism… (p. 33)

Ross, Mathison, and Vinson further argue that despite all the rhetoric about how "the Common Core offers a more progressive, student-centered, constructivist approach to learning as opposed to the 'drill and kill' test prep and scripted curriculum of NCLB," once the "tests for the Common Core" are implemented, such possibilities will quickly dissipate (p. 34). At the elementary level, the Common Core State Standards have placed such an overemphasis on math and reading scores that, researchers are finding a reduction of social studies instruction. We might note that the Common Core is a more aggressive attack on the social studies as compared with NCLB. Sadly, what E. Wayne Ross (2000) has identified as a traditional social studies instruction would actually be an improvement because it at least involves critique. What limited space for social studies NCLB and Race to the Top's overemphasis on math and reading has left intact is being assaulted by Koch brother-style activism, stocking school boards with rightist ideologues who then launch censorship campaigns. Recently in Jefferson County, Colorado, attacks on AP history are telling. It is apparently no secret that college-prep classes are one of the only places where critical thinking takes place. And from a traditional point of view, too much theory or analysis that helps students understand the reasons behind certain phenomena disrupts the presentation of "the facts speaking for themselves," constituting nothing less than an educational crisis (Rikowski, 2014).

This attack on critical thinking and social studies via the Common Core and other right-wing education reforms is focused on public schools, and this is a crucial—if obvious—insight. It helps to explain one of the contradictions of the creative economy, in which calls "to unleash creativity and innovation in educational contexts appear to stand in tension with the realities of the reorganization of education along the lines of privatization, audits and testing, standardization, and the marginalization of the social sciences" (Means, 2013, p. 55). At a general level of abstraction, there is absolutely a contradiction between standardization and creativity in education policy, practice, research, and rhetoric. Yet upon closer examination, we find that the contradiction is not operative *within* particular classes; it is rather the working classes that are subjected to standardized curricula, while bourgeois students are taught critical thinking, creativity, and so on. Private schools, in fact, are capitalizing on the popular hatred of the standards movement. One private school in

Syracuse, New York, for example, advertises on billboards by saying that it is "uncommon to the core."

The larger context is a capitalist system defined by irreconcilable antagonisms, unsolvable contradictions, and systemic crises. Any serious engagement in critical thinking runs the risk of coming to similar conclusions, which might lead to more than just thinking. Thus, these skills must be limited to the ruling class. We want students to do more than just think, and this is precisely why Marx is needed now more than ever. The attacks on the social studies are a part of a more general assault on humanity and the production of the system of nature. Consequently, those who rely on a wage to survive have been demonized as "entitled" and spoiled with things like a living wage (i.e., a wage equal to what is necessary to keep the human body alive to sell itself for another day) and, like in previous eras, are now under a generalized assault globally.

Neoliberal ideology has eroded support for the welfare state by attacking the notion of the common good as pathological or a sign of weakness. The ideology of the vile maxim, *all for self nothing for anybody else*, dominates. Gloves are off just as in earlier times, like when the English public was turned against labor, unleashing a "cynical recklessness" and a "terrorist energy" as capital's internal drive and restless hunger for surplus-value is increasingly freed from fetters or regulation. This insatiable drive for surplus-value is brought to life with the subtle shift in focus from a commodity's use-value to its exchange-value. Because surplus-value is theoretically infinite, so the length of the working day, as far as capitalism is concerned, should be pushed to its natural limits. The Marxist approach to the social studies we are presenting here starts with the realization that without external restraint or regulation, capital's drive to forever increase the portion of the working day dedicated to the accumulation of surplus labor-hours will work labor to death and exhaust the globe. This helps us better understand why ideology is so important to capital. That is, the true werewolf spirit and intention of the internal logic of capital must be kept disguised and hidden beneath the surface of deceptively equal exchanges between buyers and sellers taking place in global markets in every millisecond of every day.

The above analysis presents a major challenge to notions of social justice *within* capitalism that suggest that exploitation is the result of greed, prejudice, and bias. This approach conflates the economic drive of exploitation that is indifferent to the particular identities of laborers with the ideological mechanisms that justify exploitation that lead to unequal outcomes. The surface appearance of unequal outcomes has led to the belief that social justice can be achieved within capitalism by tinkering with distribution, ensuring equal educational opportunities or equal rights for democratic citizenship. However, racism and sexism, for example, are only employed to the extent that they contribute to the insatiable quest for surplus-value, even though once employed and internalized by society, they take on a life of their own. Toward these ends, the capitalist seeks to always increase the rate of exploitation, which is determined by the ratio of surplus labor to necessary labor.

The Marxist social studies advanced here begins with the insight that to capital, all men and women are equal. The objective goal is to accumulate as many surplus labor-hours as possible, irrespective of who produced them or under what conditions. In this context, the capitalist state relies more heavily on intensified ideological management to culturally devalue producers to not only justify exploitation but suppress the potential social unrest of laborers like the "...slaves who have at last got behind the secret of slavery and broken out in rebellion" (Marx, 1875/2002, p. 15). In this context, a Revolutionary Marxist Social Studies offers students the intellectual tools needed to uncover the mysticism of bourgeois ideology and discover the hidden process of value augmentation that leads to a tendency to work workers to death, offering a rigorous place of departure to better understand the current crisis of capital and to struggle for a communist alternative.

· 5 ·

TEACHING FERGUSON, TEACHING *CAPITAL*: SLAVERY AND THE "TERRORIST ENERGY" OF CAPITAL

A critical pedagogy of becoming harnesses the present moment, looks to history to grasp the forces determining the present, and links it with social struggles in an effort to push the configuration of the present beyond its breaking point. In this chapter, we give an example of such a process by turning to the recent nonindictments of killer cops Darren Wilson and Daniel Pantaleo. As a result of these developments—and the generalized state violence against people of color—critical educators across the U.S. and the globe are bringing the pressing topics of police brutality, state violence, and people's resistance movements into the classroom. In this chapter, we contribute to these efforts by arguing that the deadly and unpunished police violence against African Americans requires not only an awareness of slavery but an analysis of the relationship between capitalism and slavery and the subsequent subsumption of racism and white supremacy within capitalism. We use the name Ferguson in the chapter as a symbol of the daily occurrence of police violence that dates back to at least the end of the Civil War and the terrorist policing of newly "freed" slaves.

In this chapter, we more explicitly connect our critical pedagogy of becoming to street-based movements. The purpose of this analysis is to contribute to the anticapitalist undertones that exist within the current movement against police brutality. These new street movements were generated spontaneously by the state-sanctioned police murders of Michael Brown and Eric Garner, but they are expressions of a much more generalized repression in Black, Latino, and working-class communities across the United States. According to "Operation Ghetto Storm," a 2013 report by the Malcolm X Grassroots Movement, a Black person in the U.S. is killed every 28 hours by police, security guards, and vigilantes.[1] Statistical analyses by ProPublica show that Black men are 21 times more likely to be shot by police than white men.[2] While this rate of murder is alarmingly high, it is also the regular brutality, harassment, and degradation inflicted by police on people of color, people with disabilities, queers, and other oppressed groups in society that have catapulted the rebellions currently taking place in the U.S. Racism and white supremacy are not surface features of U.S. society; they are structural features that are engrained materially and ideologically. Indeed, Joe R. Feagin and Karyn D. McKinney (2002) have demonstrated that racism "generates major barriers to the full health and well-being of African Americans" in that it carries "personal, psychological, and physical costs" (p. 8). Feagin demonstrates that "physical reactions to racial discrimination often take the form of all-day headaches, stomach problems, chest pains, stress diabetes, and hypertension" (p. 31).

In this chapter, we focus particularly on the relationship between race and capitalism. What we see below is that a review of the evidence suggests that movements of the 21st century must take as their center a critique of capital, which provides the larger context that informs the manifestation of bourgeois ideology from white supremacy, patriarchy, and homophobia to the blatant disregard for the health of the world's vital ecosystems. This chapter, then, provides another example of the contribution that a critical pedagogy of becoming can make not only to classrooms but to broader social and (potentially) revolutionary movements. At the end of the chapter we offer the concept of national oppression—and its history in the international communist movement—as a useful way to understand and resist racialized capitalism.

Higher Education and Racialization

Arguing that white supremacy, racism, and the deadly devaluing and criminalization of Black life can be traced back to the long legacy of anti Blackness propagated to justify slavery is an important but incomplete insight. That is, the vicious and dehumanizing racism advanced by European slavers to justify slavery became deadly, outlined below, only when cotton became an international commodity, propelling slavery into the process of the self-expansion of capital. Capitalism, this analysis suggests, continues to be the force driving the deadliness of white supremacy in the contemporary context. But before capitalism exerted its deadly influence on slavery, white supremacy and anti-African sentiments were already being advanced as an apology for the actions of the *man-stealers* of Europe. Institutions of higher education, such as Harvard, were established *by* the elite *for* the elite during America's colonial era to advance this agenda of racialization.

For example, in his widely acclaimed *Ebony & Ivy: Race, Slavery, and the Troubled History of America's Universities*, Craig Steven Wilder (2013) begins his text noting that "Harvard's history was inseparable from the history of slavery and the slave trade" (p. 3). One of the primary purposes of higher education was to continually advance the ideological justifications for slavery and train the elites who would manage the system. Explaining what this most undemocratic purpose of higher education looked like in practice, Wilder's account is explicit: "The academy...popularized the language of race, providing intellectual cover for the social and political subjugation of non-white peoples" (ibid.). A Harvard Anatomy and Surgery professor between 1809 and 1847, John Collins Warren, taught "that in physical development, cultural accomplishment, and intellectual potential, Black people sat at the bottom of humanity" (ibid.). Situating this purpose of education in the larger context of the social and economic order dominated by slavery, Wilder explains how "college initiated" young white male elites:

> ...into the slave regimes of the Atlantic world. The founding, financing, and development of higher education in the colonies were thoroughly intertwined with the economic and social forces that transformed West and Central Africa through the slave trade and devastated indigenous nations in the Americas. The academy was a beneficiary and defender of these processes. College graduates exploited these links for centuries. They apprenticed under the slave traders of New England, the Mid-Atlantic, and Europe. They migrated to the south and to the West Indies for careers as teachers, ministers, lawyers, doctors, politicians, merchants and planters... The antebellum south represented a field of opportunity, where the wealth of the cotton planters was funding the expansion of the educational infrastructure. (pp. 1–2)

It is important to note that this purpose of education did not arise spontaneously from faculty but from the elite investor class responsible for the establishment and ongoing profitability of the colonies themselves. In other words, education was subordinated to the interests of the ruling classes.

The Marriage of Capitalism and Racism

As if the devastating and long-lasting effects of biological racism were not enough, the internal drive and spirit of capital further propelled the atrocities of slavery in America deeper into the truly horrific and genocidal. When speaking of the crimes associated with human slavery, it might be helpful to break up the practice into two parts, as has been customary—the practice of capturing and transporting human cargo and the use of the labor capacity of the slave. As might be expected, the influence of capitalism increased the atrocities in both parts.

Commenting on the use of slave labor, Marx (1867/1983) notes that before the invention of the cottongin—a piece of labor-saving technology that dramatically increased the efficiency of the tedious work of processing cotton, which involves separating the seeds from the fibers—Southern slavery was directed at "immediate local consumption" (p. 226). The cotton gin is credited to Eli Whitney, but Herbert Aptheker (1974) suggests that a skilled slave constructed the original schematics for the gin. Prior to the cotton gin, however, there was no incentive or gain to be accrued by working slaves to death. However, as the cotton gin dramatically reduced the value of labor with the notable decrease in the amount of slave labor-hours needed to process a given quantity of cotton, the productivity of slavery skyrocketed, leading to an intensified engagement with the international market (which was initially established by the slave trade itself). For example, the world's primary productive consumer of raw cotton at the time, England, saw an increase in the consumption of this material from 13,000 to about 3½ million bales from 1781 to 1860 (Du Bois, 1896/2007). British capitalists accumulated slave-labor cotton from the American South, combined it with British labor power, and forced the subsequent cotton goods on India and China chiefly through military force. North American merchants began amassing fortunes as slave vendors before 1800 and built an industrial superpower off of slave cotton after 1820. The surge in wealth and potential for even more returns had the corrupting effect of further barbarizing a practice already deeply entrenched in dehumanization.

Outside the American South, however, the production of surplus labor took hold much earlier. For example, in his classic work on slavery and the

Haitian Revolution, C.L.R. James (1963) describes the horrific production of sugar cane in the Caribbean. What the tropics provide agricultural production that more northern climates do not is a never-ending, year-round growing season. Since the slave, in slavery, is part of the means if production, the slave master must keep his slave alive and ready to labor when the growing season resumes. The productive growing season must be so productive that the slave not only reproduces the value of his own labor during the growing season but the value of his labor during the off season when the slaves' labor capacity is inactive/unproductive, as well as the value of his masters' existence, and finally, an excess value or a profit. In the Caribbean where the slave's labor is never subjected to a period of inactivity, its capacity to augment surplus-value is greatly enhanced. The insatiable demand for sugar and the capacity to produce it led to vast atrocities in the Caribbean, first the genocide of the indigenous communities, the Arawaks and others, and then the premature exhaustion and death of the enslaved African, Irish, and other imported human means of production. Indeed, "the sugar plantations demanded an acting and ceaseless labor" because "the reaping of one crop was the signal for the immediate digging of ditches and the planting of another" (James, 1963, p. 10). Consequently, the enslaved "...struggled with overwork and its usual complement—underfeeding" (p. 11). The human implements were so devalued, in fact, that "...in years of scarcity the Negroes died in thousands, epidemics broke out, the slaves fled into the woods and plantations were ruined" (ibid.).

It is what Marx (1867/1983) identified as the cynical recklessness and terrorist energy that continues to inform the internal logic and intent of capital that led to the atrocities described above and what has always driven slaves and wage laborers to rebel, from the Caribbean plantation of the 16th century to Ferguson in the 21st century. Explaining the savage nature of social control common to Caribbean cane plantations, James (1963) is descriptively explicit and theoretically precise:

> To cow them into the necessary docility and acceptance necessitated a regime of calculated brutality and terrorism, and it is this that explains the unusual spectacle of property-owners apparently careless of preserving their property: they first had to ensure their own safety. For the least fault the slaves received the harshest punishment...slaves were not unfrequently whipped to death...The slaves received the whip with more certainty and regularity than they received their food. It was the incentive to work and the guardian of discipline. (p. 12)

However, gifts of nature, the labor-saving technology, and the forced-open international market were not the only conditions necessary for the manifestation of these developments in both the American South and the Caribbean. The ability to not only replace but expand his human means of production—that is, access to new slave labor—required ever new supplies of captives. James painstakingly documents the murderous barbarity of the slave trade itself, even before the deadly influence of industrial capitalism, and he comments:

> The stockades of grinning skulls, the human sacrifices, the selling of their own children as slaves, these horrors were the product of an intolerable pressure on the African peoples, which became fiercer through the centuries as the demands of industry increased and the methods of coercion were perfected. (p. 7)

Expanding upon this conclusion, this indictment of capitalism, with a vivid example of the deadliness to which capital drove the *man stealers* in their practice of slave trading, James here is worth quoting at length:

> The slaves were collected in the interior…Marched the long journey to the sea… The weak and sickly dropping to die in the African jungle…At the slave ports they were penned into "trunks" for the inspection of the buyers. Night and day thousands of human beings were packed in these "dens of putrefaction" so no European could stay in them for longer than a quarter of an hour without fainting. The Africans fainted and recovered, or fainted and died, the mortality in the "trunks" being over 20 per cent. Outside in the harbour, waiting to empty the "trunks" as they filled, was the captain of the slave ship…waiting to enrich British capitalism with the profits of another valuable cargo…On the ships the slaves were packed in the hold on galleries one above the other…The close proximity of so many naked human beings…turned these holds into a hell…To the slave-traders they were articles of trade and no more. A captain held up by calms or adverse winds was known to have poisoned his cargo. Another killed some of his slaves to feed the others…They died not only from regime but from grief and rage and despair. (pp. 7–9)

James leaves no question that every stage in the process of the slave trade—from capturing to holding to the trans-Atlantic transport to market for sale—was just as dehumanizing and potentially deadly as the next. What James and Marx therefore demonstrate is that capitalism intensified a practice already unmoved by extreme human degradation and the genocidal depopulation of a continent. Turning back to the use of slave labor as compared with wage labor, Marx (1867/1983) again reminds us of the uniquely deadly impulse of the capitalistic process of accumulating surplus-value: "we heard how over-work thinned the ranks of the bakers in London. Nevertheless, the London labor-market is always overstocked with German and other candidates for death in the bakeries" (p. 267). Describing the operation of this phenomenon in the Caribbean, James (1963) writes that the slaves "could not replenish their numbers by reproduction," as the production of surplus-value in this context "killed them off fast. The planters deliberately worked them to death rather than wait for children to grow up" (p. 14). Explaining how this principle operated within slave labor, Marx (1867/1983) is instructive:

> ...When his [the enslaved] place can at once be supplied from foreign preserves, the duration of his life becomes a matter of less moment than its productiveness while it lasts. It is accordingly a maxim of slave management, in slave-importing countries, that the most effective economy is that which takes out of the human chattel in the shortest space of time the utmost amount of exertion it is capable of putting forth. (p. 266)

Again, this development represents the barbaric and deadly shift that always accompanies unfettered capitalism: "it was no longer a question of obtaining from him a certain quantity of useful products. It was now a question of the production of surplus-labor itself" (Marx, 1867/1983, p. 236).

This is not an insignificant transformation. The impulse to accumulate surplus labor, the substance of surplus-value, can never be stilled, that is, there can never be too much money. This drive for profit—especially when unregulated—not only leads to the premature exhaustion and death of the laborer but also to the rapid (absolute or relative) physical or geographical expansion of the means and mode of production as well. As a result, the whole of the South was transformed into a vast region of cotton fields, and it became more profitable to work slaves to death than to take care of them into old age. The drive to expand slave territory was fueled by the accumulation of surplus-value. Marx consequently understood all too well that the South's 300,000 slave owners were not really fighting to break the Union to preserve a traditional way of life mutually beneficial to all involved, both freeman and slave (5 million white laborers and 3 million enslaved Blacks). Rather, they sought to preserve the Union, converting it into a vast slave nation oligarchy. Contrary to critical race theory that takes white supremacy as a political system of racial privilege (Cole, 2009), the desire to extend the white supremacist slave state was not determined by race but by the accumulation of surplus-value. However, this does not suggest that the capitalist is aware of surplus-value itself. The slaver, like the capitalist in general, simply "...wishes to receive as much labor as possible for as little money as possible" (Marx, 1867/1983, p. 541). However, race and class here are not separate entities as interpretations of Marx's notion of the base and superstructure would suggest. That is, the base—the economy—and the superstructure—various cultural formations designed to serve the interests of the base—are not separate and distinct but rather absolutely inseparable.

During the Civil War, Marx supported the Union against slavery. However, he critiqued Lincoln for being too soft on the slavers. Marx believed the North should have taken a more revolutionary position in the Civil War and encouraged and supported the slaves in a rebellion against their masters. Marx celebrated the abolition movement even while arguing it should take a more straightforward position against capitalism. Marx saw the labor movement of white freemen and the struggle of the enslaved against slavery as one and the same. Aware of the ways in which poor whites and Blacks were intentionally kept apart, Marx was adamant that the biggest barrier to the complete emancipation of all laborers, free and enslaved alike, was white, working-class racism. In fact, Marx saw this divisive force as the primary factor degrading the gains against capital laborers could have made in the aftermath of the Civil War (Marx, 2007). It is not at all an exaggeration, we believe, to claim that the biases and prejudice of white workers in the U.S. continue to play a crucial role in capital's global domination.

Yet according to bourgeois ideology—which always presents itself as a non perspective, or as "just the way it is"—capitalism is the path to freedom and equality. Given this normalized idea, which informs the view that before 1865, slavery was the only barrier to freedom in the U.S., it is not intuitive that the introduction of capitalism would lead to the escalation of atrocities within slavery. Dominant historical narratives teach us just the opposite. That is, the historical narrative American students tend to be uncritically reared on is that once slavery was abolished, capitalism could begin spreading its freedom and equality southward, gradually chipping away at the white supremacist ideological residue of a bygone era standing as a fading barrier to meritocracy. Challenging the core of this ideology, Marx's discussion of the internal logic of capital makes it absolutely clear that the logic is a dangerous and deadly one, which continues to inform the deadliness of white supremacy. This logic, which we have explained in previous chapters, leads to the general drive to push down the value of labor-power and extend the working day to its natural limits.

Ideologically, this drive to lower the value of labor-power results in the value of the laborer's subjective social being becoming devalued. This can result in low self-esteem, self-hatred, and even the worship of the ruling class by the working class. This can happen despite the fact that many of the labor-saving technologies that drive down the value of labor-power are actually produced by workers through the production process (i.e., forms of cooperation). However—and this is where education can play a pivotal role—the result among workers conscious of the capitalist system is deep resentment and either cynicism and despair or organization and revolution. The most exaggerated examples of the tendency to culturally devalue the working class are the ways anti-Black racism has been employed to justify dramatically increasing the rate of exploitation of and unemployment in Black communities. In times of crisis and recession, the Black worker, consequently, is always the first to be laid off. As a result, today, generally speaking, the Black family is 22 times more likely to be in poverty than the white family.

A major force driving this condition is the use of the hourly wage. While struggles over the length of the working day in previous eras were motivated by workers literally being worked to death, the suffering Marx (1867/1983) first pointed to in regard to the hourly wage stems from the laborer's "insufficient employment" (p. 546). If the hourly wage is based upon "…the quotient of the value of a day's labor-power, divided by the number of hours of the average working day," then underemployment destroys the material basis upon which the "unit-measure for time-wages" is based. That is, if the capitalist only hires the laborer for a portion of the day or week, then the price of labor "loses all meaning" because it is based upon "a definite number of hours" (ibid.). Consequently:

> The connection between the paid and unpaid labor is destroyed. The capitalist can now wring from the laborer a certain quantity of surplus-labor without allowing him the labor-time for his own subsistence. He can annihilate all regularity of employment, and according to his own convenience, caprice, and the interest of the moment, make the most enormous over-work alternate with relative or absolute cessation of work. He can, under the pretense of paying "the normal price of labor," abnormally lengthen the working day without any corresponding compensation to the laborer. (ibid.)

The lowering of the price of labor-power by extending the length of the workday inevitably results in one laborer doing the work of perhaps two workers while "the supply of labor on the market remains constant" (p. 549). As a result, competition among laborers intensifies, and the capitalist is able to continue to drive down wages below what is necessary for the laborer to reproduce his existence for another day's work. Eventually, access to these abnormal quantities of surplus labor-hours becomes a source of competition between capitalists. Explaining this complicated process, Marx is instructive:

> A part of the price of the commodity consists of the price of labor. The unpaid part of the labor-price need not be reckoned in the price of the commodity. It may be presented to the buyer. This is the first step to which competition leads. The second step to which it drives, is to exclude also from the selling price of the commodity, at least a part of the abnormal surplus-value created by the extension of the working-day. In this way an abnormally low selling price of the commodity arises, at first sporadically, and becomes fixed by degrees; a lower selling price which henceforth becomes the constant basis of a miserable wage for an excessive working-time, as originally it was the product of these very circumstances. (ibid.)

The ways in which capitalists have complained to the courts concerning the unpaid labor-hours of their competitors reveals just how unaware the capitalist is of surplus labor-time, for even in the paid hours of labor, there exists an unpaid portion. Capitalists tend to be unaware that the accumulation of these unpaid portions of each labor hour employed is the source of their own profit. For the capitalist, then, the system of wage labor has a basis in fairness. The existence of racism and prejudice also contributes to the belief in bourgeois society that individuals receive the value of their inherent worth in both wages and access to jobs. In this context, the capitalist, like the laborer, tends not to see the exploitation that operates below the surface or the prejudice that leads to the average privilege of white, male workers over all others.

The white worker's greater access to jobs includes access to police jobs. White workers tend to hold the police jobs not only in white working-class neighborhoods but in Black ones as well. With the exaggerated devaluing and demonization of people of color, and in particular Black and Latino youth, it is not surprising that white cops kill youth of color at alarming rates with near impunity. This is a legacy that can be traced back to the era when the productive use of slave labor became much more lethal. But serving the purpose of the necessary ideological mechanisms described above is the very process of capitalist circulation itself and the use of the money relation. Making this point, and using slavery as a contrasting example strengthening the impact of his argument, Marx explains with biting precision:

In slave-labor, even that part of the working-day in which the slave is only replacing the value of his own means of existence, in which, therefore, in fact, he works for himself alone, appears as labor for his master. All the slave's labor appears as unpaid labor. In wage-labor, on the contrary, even surplus-labor, or unpaid labor, appears as paid. There the property relation conceals the labor of the slave for himself; here the money-relation conceals the unrequited labor of the wage-laborer. (pp. 539–540)

The exploitation of outright slavery is apparent at the surface level. It is the more hidden mechanisms of exploitation under wage labor that help us understand why renowned historian Eric Foner (1988), in his award-winning book *Reconstruction: America's Unfinished Revolution, 1867–1877*, concluded that "for [B]lacks, the abolition of slavery meant...an end to unrequited toil" (p. 103). Of course the planter class warned that Blacks, without slavery and thus left to their own devices, would not work and their idleness would destroy the country. In response, slaves seemed to agree that their labor had in fact built the nation, and the true idle class could be found among the wealthiest of the slavers. For many former slaves, wage labor represented a departure from unrequited labor, even though within the wage system, a part of each requited hour of work contains an unrequited portion. However, the transitional experience of being a slave, a part of the means of production, one year, and an owner of a commodity (i.e., labor-power) the very next year gave some former slaves a unique window into the hidden exploitation of wage labor: "Blacks resented being offered as annual wages sums far below what planters had paid before the Civil War to rent slaves for the year. ('The Negro...' a Union army officer commented, 'thought it strange he was not worth as much as before.')" (p. 107).

In the highly racialized context of U.S. slavery, it is not surprising that many former slaves conceptualized freedom as "freedom from white control," which, for many, meant having direct access to land as the final act of independence (pp. 103–104). While economic independence afforded by small landownership has proven far from capable of resisting the encroachment and expansion of monopoly industrial capitalism, which gained momentum after the Civil War, the distribution of former slave plantations to their former slaves—despite the legitimate argument for it—was bitterly resisted and successfully subverted by the former class of wealthy slavers. It is no wonder, then, that there was so much white ruling-class pushback against this conception of freedom after the abolition of slavery in the U.S. in 1865 based upon an agrarian land reform that might be thought of as a mild form of reverse primitive accumulation. The transition from chattel slavery to wage slavery was assisted by not only the very structure of capitalism itself and its false sense of equality and freedom but by a form of capitalist, industrial education as well. The transition from slavery to wage labor was relatively easy even though there was significant pushback from former slaves who knew all too well that being compelled to sell their labor to their former masters represented anything but freedom. Mandatory ignorance laws, part of the Black Codes, enforced after a series of slave revolts in its deadly era of value augmentation, resulted in a deep sense among former slaves that education possessed some liberatory potential.

Freedmen Bureau Commissioner General Oliver Howard, essentially in charge of Reconstruction after the Civil War, saw education as playing a central role in the transition to a conception of freedom that must be defined and defended against subversion. According to Foner, "education, for General Howard, was the foundation upon which all efforts to assist the freedmen rested, and the encouragement and oversight of schools for blacks occupied a significant portion of local agents' time" (p. 144). These educational efforts were spearheaded by white northern missionaries, many of whom held racist attitudes toward the freedmen and who viewed their work paternalistically, believing that they were helping people unable to help or care for themselves. While the American Missionary Association (AMA) attempted to discourage their teachers from overt racism, the American Freedman's Union Commission trained as many Black teachers as they could. Together with the Freedman's Bureau, the American Freedman's Association established the first Black colleges in the South dedicated to teacher preparation. The role Historically Black Colleges and Universities (HBCUs) have played in the post-Civil War struggle for liberation should not be surprising:

> Public HBCUs became epicenters in the struggle for human rights…shaping the destiny of America. Driven by a tenaciously segregated society, the students and faculty joined hands with religious and civic leaders and moved the entire nation toward a new level of social consciousness. The story of public HBCUs is a story of a people liberated through education [and] empowered through political action…They serve as laboratories where solutions to issues facing the Black community are addressed. (Payne, 2013, pp. 15–16)

With the official end of slavery in the U.S. in 1865, the material wealth generated by slave labor in the cotton kingdom had already been amassed and used to develop and expand the machine factory throughout the North. Former slaves were at the forefront of Reconstruction and the rise of the HBCU.

In the hands of former slaves, it is not surprising that HBCUs eventually came to play a central role in the Civil Rights movement. Of course, the changing needs of capital as industrialization progressed led to the Morrill Acts and Land Grant Universities, institutions that were charged with advancing mechanical arts, military science, and agricultural technologies. These grants provided the incentive for the expansion of systems of higher education from the perspective of capital. However, one of the reasons HBCUs were excluded from these education funds for higher education was that Black colleges did not begin to be recognized as operating at a college level until the beginning of the 20th century. Biological racism certainly played a significant role in this refusal of status, but the legacy of enforced ignorance laws during slavery led to early Black colleges focusing on elementary- and secondary-level instruction. After gradually receiving collegiate status and access to public funds; after a series of student and faculty protests achieved a racially representative administration, and after the 1954 *Brown v. Board* decision that paved the way for more open access in America's standard, white-dominated institutions, "the question of why [B]lack colleges were still needed began to flourish" (Young, 2013, p. 46).

In the neoliberal era, it is equally not surprising that in the attack on public higher education, HBCUs have suffered first and the most, as a general rule. Providing more insight regarding this trend Payne (2013) paints a larger context noting that, "mis-education, poverty, and the absence of a national investment in HBCUs magnify inequality in American society. Structural barriers are created to systematically exclude Black colleges from the vast resources obligated to 'federally sponsored' universities" (p. 29). Despite the challenges faced by HBCUs in the 21st century, they continue to offer vital spaces for organizing work and the necessary innovation it requires:

> HBCUs offer a more supportive collegiate environment [as compared with mainstream institutions]…thereby enhancing overall academic experience…Black students at HBCU campuses have more freedom to concentrate on academic studies… without having to struggle with institutional bigotry and overt and subtle racism from other students, faculty, or administrators. (Young, 2013, p. 47)

In the street protests spontaneously emerging around the U.S. focused on the state's deadly assault on Black lives, the HBCU campus will surely continue to offer a safe space for organizing, building theoretical arguments, and developing tactics to push the quest for freedom beyond bourgeois limitations. The logic, of course, subverting the complete emancipation of labor in general and

Black lives in particular is an insatiable appetite for the accumulation of sur-plus-value. The murder of Black youth at the hands of white cops only mirrors the ways in which the werewolf within capital has been unleashed with a savage barbarity on Black communities. The larger context, of course, is a declining system of global capital that must repress those elements of the working class that have historically been the most revolutionary and militant.

Through the bourgeoisie's doctrinal system, laborers are socialized to be-lieve that capitalism is the true path to freedom and equality. The laws of exchange are supposed to guarantee this. That is, unlike the prejudice and bias driving aristocratic feudalism and slavery, buyers and sellers under cap-italism meet on the market as equals. From this perspective, the exchange between labor, the seller of labor power, and capital, the purchaser of labor power, is fair. Labor, after all, willingly sells their product on the market, and the capitalist purchases it for its market value. The products that are created by the laborer do not belong to the seller but to the purchaser, the capitalist. No coercion or exploitation exists within this exchange, as far as the buyer is concerned. But, as we have mentioned, the price and value of labor-power is always the result of class struggle. From the perspective of the class con-scious laborer, the productive consumption of her labor power is fundamen-tally based on a hidden process of accumulation or exploitation. Capitalism is in fact based exclusively on this drive to augment as much surplus-value as possible, and when unfettered or unregulated, it inevitably leads to the pre-mature exhaustion and death of the laborer. Rather than freedom and equal-ity—outside of the freedom of the capitalist to exploit and the laborer to be exploited or excluded—what capitalism offers is social misery and degradation fueled by a slew of unmet needs and a deadly white supremacy informed by the same "cynical recklessness" and "terrorist energy" that Marx witnessed in the 19th century. The fight against murderous white supremacy at the heart of America's bourgeois society is at the same time the fight against the *terrorist* process of value augmentation unique to capitalism.

National Oppression and Resistance

Capital, as Marx constantly reminds us, is not a thing but a social relation. Resistance is thus *internal* to capital. One of the primary tasks of the critical educator is to foster this resistance, in terms of consciousness, subjectivity, and organization. What we have been witnessing in the streets of many American cities has been a tremendous display of this spontaneous resistance to oppression and exploitation. Perhaps history will show that the non indictments of Wilson and Pantaleo were small sparks that lit the prairie ablaze. There are many factors that will determine this potentiality, however. We believe that one of these factors is the way in which we understand police brutality, racism, and capitalism. If we see police brutality as accidental to the system, and if we see racism as merely a leftover from slavery, then the burgeoning resistance movement will undoubtedly exhaust itself, collapsing under the weight of ideological mystifications. If police brutality and racism are seen as endemic to the capitalist production and augmentation of value, however, then the street rebellions we are witnessing could translate into a broad-based, national mass movement striking at capital itself. In this closing section, we want to offer one final connection between capitalism and racism, one that has important implications for organizing: the concept of national oppression.

Just like every worker in the U.S. is taught that the overthrow of the slavocracy in the South gave way to capitalism's attendant equalities and freedoms, so too every worker learns that the U.S. is a nation. Schools have students recite that the U.S. is "one nation" on a daily basis. This assertion, however, is as false as it is commonplace. The U.S. is instead a country that contains within it many oppressed nations, including the Black nation and hundreds of Indigenous or First Nations, many of whom continue to struggle for their own national sovereignty.

The national question was first broached by Marx in relation to Ireland and the struggle of Irish workers. Initially, Marx believed that Ireland would be liberated by the struggle of workers in the colonial power, England. Marx changed his position, however, after taking into account the anti-Irish racism that was deep seated in the English working-class. Instead of relying on workers in the colonizing country to liberate the colony, Marx called on English workers to support Ireland's right to self-determination. Lenin took up and advanced this line in relation to Czarist Russia, which, at the time of the Bolshevik Revolution in 1917, was referred to as a "prison house of nations," in that Russia contained hundreds of nationalities and languages. These oppressed nations within Russia suffered a higher rate of exploitation as well as cultural oppression. By viewing these entities as oppressed nations, Lenin and the Bolsheviks were able to move beyond the mere calls to "unite the working class" and were able to pay particular attention to particular forms of oppression. It is no coincidence, then, that racial and national relations within the Soviet Union were greatly advanced, especially when compared to the U.S.

This is never mentioned in U.S. schools, of course, because it disrupts the capitalist narrative of the Soviet Union as an "authoritarian" or "totalitarian" state. While there were definitely authoritarian elements within the Soviet Union's complex history (and within any country's history, for that matter), it is crucial to acknowledge the important gains made for the majority of workers and oppressed people.

The Marxist and Leninist conception of national oppression has visceral resonances with the situation in the U.S. today. There is, additionally, a lineage of the left that has viewed the U.S. as a multinational state—as a state, that is, that contains within it oppressed nations, including the Black nation. Black communist militant Harry Haywood was one of the most prominent figures in articulating the position of a Black nation inside the U.S. Working in collaboration with Bolsheviks, Haywood formulated the "Black Belt" thesis, which held that Black people constituted an oppressed nation within the U.S. Black people constituted a nation because they were "set apart by a common ethnic origin, economically interrelated in various classes, united by a common historical experience, reflected in a special culture and psychological makeup" (Haywood, 1978, p. 232), in addition to holding a contiguous territory stretching across the South. As such, Black people in the U.S. had a right to national self-determination. This position was eventually adopted by the entire communist movement at the 6th Congress of the Third International in 1928.

As a matter of historical record, it is quite remarkable that as far back as 1928, communists and communist parties across the world were fighting for the right of Black people in the U.S. to self-determination. Yet they were not doing so out of a desire for separatism. Ultimately, they wanted all races and nations to unite on a class basis. By emphasizing national oppression and the rights of oppressed nations to self-determination, however, communists were able to pay particular attention to the ways in which some people are super-oppressed and exploited and to how the bourgeoisie were able to extract even more surplus labor-time from these populations. This position was also intended to combat the racism and national chauvinism engrained in white U.S. workers. And, in addition to serving as a means to agitate against calls for integration into U.S. capitalist society, it allowed Haywood to think more precisely through the relationship between reform and revolution. In *For a Revolutionary Position on the Negro Question*, written in 1958, four years after the *Brown v. Board of Education* decision, Haywood reminded the Communist Party USA of its position and railed against the CPUSA for following the NAACP's "bourgeois assimilationist" position. Haywood wrote:

While we Communists fight for every possible democratic demand of the Negro people, and welcome all advances made, we have pointed out that the Negro question is at bottom the question of an oppressed nation in the South and a national minority in the North.

Here, Haywood is saying that reform and revolution are not mutually exclusive. Yes, we should fight for judicial reforms, but we must have no illusions as to their ultimate effectiveness. Haywood went on to rail against the leadership of the CPUSA:

With the outlawing of the segregation of schools by the Supreme Court in May of 1954, the right-revisionist trend in our Party unreservedly embraced the pro-imperialist swindle of imminent, peaceful, democratic "integration" of the Negro people into all aspects of American life.

This was two years after Khrushchev's "secret speech," in which he denounced the entirety of Stalin's leadership and which marked a definitive rightward turn for the international communist movement. What is most notable, however, is the way in which Haywood is able to support calls for reform while at the same time insisting upon revolution on a class basis.

Taking national oppression seriously in pedagogy and organizing also helps to forge crucial links between different sites and forms of oppression and resistance. Consider, for example, the beautiful display of solidarity issued by the Popular Front for the Liberation of Palestine (PFLP) in the early days of the Ferguson protests. The PFLP, founded in 1967, represents the largest grouping of Marxists and the left wing in the Palestinian Liberation Organization. On August 19, 2014, PFLP comrade Khaled Barakat issued a statement from the PFLP in solidarity with the Ferguson protesters and the Black nation in the U.S. While it is not extraordinary for such a statement to be issued in general, the particular circumstances of this statement are truly remarkable.

Michael Brown was murdered on August 9, 2014. At the time of this act of repression against the Black nation in the U.S., the Palestinian nation had been under a brutal bombardment by the occupying Israeli army for 32 days. Beginning July 8, this war against the Palestinian people would last until August 26. This entailed not only a nonstop bombing campaign against Gaza—one of the most densely populated territories of the globe—but also a ground invasion by the Israeli "Defense" Forces. This attack killed more than 2,000 Palestinians and left more than 10,000 injured and disabled. The Palestinians fought back with the weapons that they had at their disposal, with their ingenuity and their resources, and they ultimately won. With the support from Syria, Iran, and Hezbollah, they were able to defeat the much better-armed Israeli forces. The battle turned decisively in favor of the Palestinians once the Israelis entered Gaza. It turns out that they are much better at carpet bombing than they are at actual fighting. The PFLP was one of the many Palestinian groups engaged in the war (contrary to the Zionist narrative, Hamas was only one grouping in the united front effort). This means that at the same moment as comrade Barakat was extending a gesture of solidarity to the people of Ferguson, the PFLP was defending its own nation from an attack by one of the most well-armed and merciless oppressing nations in history. Barakat's comments included the following concise linkage between resistance movements in the U.S., Palestine, and internationally:

> As people in Africa, Asia, Latin America and the Arab World see the brutality of the United States outside its borders, these communities confront its racist and colonial oppression within the borders of the U.S. The two are inextricably linked… Black people in the United States are in fact under siege. And just as we demand the end of the siege on our Palestinian people, in Gaza and everywhere, we demand an end to the siege of institutionalized racism and oppression in education, jobs, social services and all areas of life, and support the Black movements struggling to end that siege…. Every victory inside the United States and political achievement by popular movements and liberation struggles is a victory for Palestine and a victory for a world of human liberation. (PFLP, Aug. 19, 2014)

The solidarity evidenced here is not purely abstract or intellectual. It is no mere statement of political agreement. Instead, this solidarity is visceral and historical, communicating clearly that the fate of oppressed nations in the U.S. is linked to the fate of oppressed nations around the world. There is also a common enemy identified: U.S. imperialism (and its proxy forces, including obviously Israel).

Additionally, organizing around national oppression ensures that we do not miss that founding and ongoing act of genocide and colonization that is the occupation of the Americas. This has been and continues to be one of the most blatant and bold acts of national oppression. It also points to one of the fundamental issues that any revolutionary movement in the U.S. must address, which is "the failure to problematize the issue of (colonized) land" (Grande, 2004, p. 49). When workers of any nationality seek justice or liberation in the U.S., they must take into account the fact that the movements themselves take place on colonized land.

The U.S. is still highly racially segregated socially, economically, and geographically. With the framework of national oppression, the images of white cops and reserve troops repressing the rebellions in Ferguson and elsewhere begin to make more sense. The ways in which the struggles against police brutality, racism, and capitalism can join together also becomes clearer in this framework. It is the duty of working-class whites not to be mere "allies" but to be *comrades* fighting for socialism and supporting the right to self-determination for Black people and all oppressed nations within the U.S. Only in this way can multinational class unity against capitalism be built, a unity that takes seriously the differences within the working class.

Notes

1. https://mxgm.org/wp-content/uploads/2013/04/Operation-Ghetto-Storm.pdf
2. http://www.propublica.org/article/deadly-force-in-black-and-white

· 6 ·

CONNECTING "ECONOMIC BONDAGE" TO "PERSONIFIED CAPITAL": ANOTHER STEP TOWARD A CRITICAL PEDAGOGY OF BECOMING

This chapter continues the development of a critical pedagogy by examining the economic bondage to capital via the capitalist. This project began with an engagement with Marx's *Philosophic Manuscripts* and with Peter McLaren's (2005) Marxist-Humanist revolutionary pedagogy. Specifically, Peter McLaren's (2005) emphasis on the process of labor transcending the labor-capital relationship and in remaking the self as non alienated labor, collectively remaking society (i.e., becoming), was the foundation from which this Marxist pedagogy of becoming has been built. Central to that project has been Marx's (1844/1988) correction of Hegel's dialectic and his conclusion that "the outstanding thing in Hegel…is…the dialectic of negativity as the moving and generating principle" (p. 149). This negation of the negation views all entities, including capitalism, as contradictory because they embody their own negation. Capitalism, that is, possesses the potential to become its opposite. If capital's true spirit and intent is to work laborers to death to maximize surplus labor-time—and therefore to dehumanize, fragment, and mangle the human being—then the opposite of this is a system that encourages the flourishing of human potential by abolishing surplus labor-time and educationally fostering the unification of mental labor and manual labor.

This chapter's contribution to a Marxist pedagogy of becoming starts with the ways in which labor's "economic bondage" under capitalist production relations developed not only out of feudalistic circuits of commodity exchange based upon the law of equivalents but out of the historical development of the capitalist himself (i.e., "personified capital"). The analysis developed in what follows more broadly relates to our insistence that we pay particular attention to the structural and systemic coordinates within and through which our subjectivities are fashioned and refashioned. In this chapter, we focus on the subjectivity of the capitalist, the living embodiment of the logic of capital. For Marx (1867/1992)—and for us—the capitalist is merely capital "endowed with consciousness and a will" (p. 151). It is the capitalist's relation to and within the mode of production that matters. This is, then, completely irrespective of any habits or characteristics that the capitalist may possess. As Marx writes in a staged conversation between the worker and the capitalist, "You may be a model citizen, perhaps a member of the Society for the Prevention of Cruelty to Animals, and in the odour of sanctity to boot; but the thing that you represent face to face with me has no heart in its breast" (p. 225).

Before we investigate the central issues of the chapter, briefly reviewing the law of equivalents is necessary. That is, under feudalism's simple circulation, money served the function of facilitating the exchange of diverse commodities, and the primary objective here was the consumption of use-values. Money, as a measurement of the cost of raw materials plus labor time, served the function of determining, for example, the equivalent value of a certain quantity of grain in relation to the value of a pair of pants. This advanced division of labor and the resulting production of commodities were necessary requirements for the emergence of capitalism because capitalism requires a separation between a product's exchange-value and use-value, especially in regard to human labor-power as a commodity. Departing from the exchange of equivalents, labor-power under capitalism produces more value than it receives in the form of the wage. Marx demonstrates how the laws of commodity production (i.e., the exchange of equivalents) developed into the laws of capitalist accumulation and subsequently became ideologically mystified as the unpaid labor hours appropriated by capital remain hidden behind the myth of equivalents. Again, this hidden process is made possible by the separation of labor-power's exchange-value and use-value.

In this chapter, the historical development of this process of expropriation is further explored. Better understanding actually existing capitalism is the basis of our approach to a Marxist critical pedagogy of becoming against and beyond the laborer's "economic bondage" to capital. Yet in actually existing capitalism, we do not come up against "capital" but against capitalists, who Marx referred to as "capital personified." In this way, it becomes clear that while the laborer is subjugated or subordinated to the capitalist, the capitalist is simultaneously subordinated or coerced by the laws of the production and expansion of capital. This chapter will add another layer of analysis to the capitalist's "cynical recklessness" and "terrorist energy" that Marx identifies as the true guiding force of capital. Because this mode of production is driven by a limitless quest for surplus-value, and because only human labor-power can produce value, there is always a tendency to extend the working day to its absolute limits unless state regulation or working-class resistance counters this tendency. A Marxist critical pedagogy of becoming looks to uncover the hidden mechanisms of capitalist production relations that might open up possibilities for revolutionizing them. In Chapter 4, we showed that educational labor has a similar effect on the student as the machine has on the production of products. The critical exception here, drawing on Rikowski's (1997, 2004, 2014) work on capital's weakest link, is that the educator—unlike the machine—is a conscious, agential being and thus has the potential to subvert the purpose and direction of education. In other words, rather than produce obedient workers, the critical pedagogue can find ways to labor toward the creation of revolution through the development of revolutionary subjectivities that are antagonistic to capital. The pedagogy developed here—and really, throughout this entire book—flips the base of our consciousness from relations of exchange to relations of production. As Neil Smith (1984/2008) writes, "If production relations under capitalism are characterized by the exploitation of labor… the exchange relations under capitalism are based on the principles of equality and freedom" (pp. 75–76). It is this latter set of relations upon which bourgeois consciousness is erected and that must be negated. Working towards these ends, we now turn, along with Marx, to a more detailed investigation of "personified capital" and its connection to the "economic bondage" and alienation of the laborer.

The Capitalist and the Laborer

Marx provides countless examples of the ways in which the laws of capitalist appropriation and expansion act as an external coercive force on the capitalist, compelling him to act in very specific ways. For example, Marx argues that the capitalist tends not to be aware of surplus-value itself. The capitalist in general, that is, simply "...wishes to receive as much labor as possible for as little money as possible" (Marx, 1867/1983, p. 541). And in the third volume of *Capital*, Marx (1894/1981) notes that profit disguises "surplus-value, a form in which its origin and the secret of its existence are veiled and obliterated. In point of fact, profit is the *form of appearance* of surplus-value" (p. 139, emphasis added). Because this analysis challenges the bourgeois idea that poverty and inequality—rather than consequences of the internal logic of capital and the laws of capitalist accumulation—are the result of greedy capitalists out of control in need of reining in, we examine relevant aspects of Marx's discussions of the capitalist who forms but one component of the antagonistic labor-capital relationship. In other words, if the inconvenience of poverty and suffering are merely reflections of the actions of some rogue individuals, then capitalism does not need to be subverted, just properly regulated or safeguarded. Neither Marx nor we are ambiguous in the insistence that the problem with capitalism is not the capitalists per se but the process of capitalist production and accumulation itself, which requires revolutionary transformation.

As we see below, because the capitalist views labor as a resource he is entitled to, he will go to war over his perceived right to exclusive access to it and the resulting capacity to accumulate wealth (part of which is surplus labor-time). Since the completion of the intellectual degradation of the laborer, signaled by the emergence of the machine factory discussed in Chapter 4, laborers are increasingly viewed and treated as the unthinking automatons required for the reproduction of capitalism and capitalist social relations of production. With the development of teacher-proof curricula and online educational platforms, even those workers who work with knowledge have been reduced to an appendage of a machine—a machine that is not commanded by teachers but rather one that commands them.

Capital will do whatever it deems necessary to resist the movement toward abolishing the possibility of expropriating surplus labor-time. Our Marxist pedagogy of becoming is grounded in the insistence that laborers should not only be requited for every minute of every hour of labor worked—thereby abolishing the basis of capital (i.e., surplus labor-time)—but also that laborers should participate in a form of critical education that engages them, from preschool on, in the development of their intellectual labor as a central part of the process of encouraging the unification of mental labor and manual labor—in short, to *become* more human and to participate more fully in the production of the system of nature. Educators, in and for a socialist alternative, must therefore be expected to work as autonomous, creative, critical scholars who are experts in not only their own particular subject area but in human developmental psychology and political economy as well. In considering what aspects of the capitalist state will persist with the abolition of surplus labor-time, education will surely not only remain, but its importance will increase due to the long legacy of intellectual degradation currently plaguing the lion's share of humanity. As demonstrated already, the alienation between manual labor and mental labor was completed by the machine factory, which displaced human muscle power with steam and electric power and, along with it, the laborer's last vestige of intellectual capacity needed to operate the tools of manufacture proper before the dominance of the machine factory.

Marx demonstrates how the laws of capitalist augmentation foster competition between capitalists, which serves as another layer of external coercion on the capitalist to perpetually search for ways to increase profit margins. The coercive laws of competition dictate that the capitalist, if he wishes to remain so, must always align his production arrangements in accordance with those that are predominant at the time. If he fails to do so, he will be driven out of business. This is precisely why appeals to more humane or equitable business practices are ultimately futile, for equitability runs counter to the coercive laws of competition. Collective action by the organized working class may win a general greater portion of the values produced in the production process, and this is an important struggle that has witnessed relevant success in history (although these struggles were most successful when there was a proletarian offensive in the global class war). But even in these situations, any reforms or gains are completely precarious and, as long as capitalism is around, temporary.

The coercive laws of competition—particularly in the beginning stages of capitalism—compel the capitalist to expand his capital by perpetually expanding variable and constant capital rather than consuming his revenue. This competitive drive between capitalists has been one of the primary forces propelling it into new eras and expanding it across the planet. Aside from the very emergence of capital itself, arguably the most significant of these transitions was the shift from manufacture proper to the machine factory. Because unfettered capitalism will always push the capitalist to exploit labor to the point of the premature exhaustion and death of the laborer, working-class resistance has been a present force pushing against capital's insatiable appetite for surplus-value since very early in capital's development. Subsequent restrictions on capital's free exploitation of labor, which took the form of regulations on the length of the working day, immediately led the cold, calculating capitalist to devise ways to increase the intensity and efficiency of the production process. This movement led to the machine factory, as the inventions of machines that could automatically and more consistently perform tasks that laborers previously performed with tools—tools powered by human muscle and controlled by human intelligence—dramatically increased the productivity of labor. In other words, with the machine, the amount of human labor it takes to convert a given quantity of constant capital into products greatly diminishes. Consequently, the amount of labor hours it takes to reproduce the value of one's daily existence also decreases. That is, because the price of a commodity is, in part, determined by the average amount of labor hours it takes to produce a given product, when a capitalist develops a new piece of labor-saving technology, that capitalist has a temporary market advantage over his or her competitors until the new technology has been fully integrated into the process of production and the average amount of labor time it takes to produce the given product has been lowered. At this point, the competitive process starts anew. This is so because the value that labor transmits to its product through the labor process does not change with fluctuations in productivity. If production becomes more productive, labor power still dispenses the same value of labor over a given period of time; it just transmits this value to a greater number of products, thereby decreasing the value of each product because each product embodies less congealed labor-power. With the machine factory, the domination of labor is complete, and profit margins accelerate to absurd levels.

Unaware of the inherent exploitation involved in the productive consumption of labor-power, the capitalist actually tends to believe his purchase of labor-power on the market is fair. That is, the capitalist sees absolutely no difference between purchasing labor-power, a machine, or a batch of raw materials or other inputs. At the same time, because the capitalist mindset tends to view labor as part of machinery and raw materials, he also tends to believe that labor is a resource he is entitled to, that is, that it "belongs to the capitalist" (Marx, 1867/1983, p. 577), even though fluctuations in the cost of living are not transferred immediately to the capitalist but to the laborer. That is, if the wage represents the average cost of minimal survival, which the laborer reproduces through a portion of his work time, then an increase in, say, the price of a foodstuff will be felt directly by labor's stomach through his or her pocket. Marx uses the example of the capitalist perspective on immigration as an example of how the capitalist views labor as a resource it is either importing or allowing/not allowing to migrate.

Another example is the way in which educators, from pre-K through higher education, are viewed as part of the educational machinery and thus as a resource that the managing entity (whether it be the state, the corporation, or a public-private hybrid) is entitled to use as it pleases. Educational labor-power, even when exploited by for-profit educational corporations, does not produce any new value. Rather, it consumes revenue or already produced value, and, like the machine, transfers its own value through the expenditure of labor (the act of teaching) to the student to produce a worker whose labor-power commodity may fetch a higher price on the market (because its production has consumed a greater number of useful labor hours). The educator's labor has therefore been a fluctuating part of the necessary non productive labor required at the current stage of development of production. In other words, the forever-transforming techniques and products of production impact the type of workers required by capital, thereby continually impacting capitalist education. It is within this context that the labor of educators is viewed by capital as just another varied and adjustable natural resource that is within its justifiable domain or sphere of influence. The human laborer, in the mind of the capitalist, has been completely dehumanized and is no longer viewed as a natural human being but instead is seen as a necessary component of the means of production. Because the capitalist is entitled to his riches, he is entitled to the necessary ingredients, including human labor-power (and ultimately the laborer herself).

The very process of production, then, which requires a class of dependents with no means to reproduce their existence outside of exchanging the value of their labor for a wage, increasingly alienates the laborer from the production of the system of nature and what it means—or could mean—to be a natural being participating fully in the production of herself and the world at large. Providing a deep understanding of this expanding alienation and subjugation within capital, Marx is not without precision:

> Capitalist production, therefore, of itself reproduces the separation between labor-power and the means of labor. It thereby reproduces and perpetuates the condition for exploiting the laborer. It incessantly forces him to sell his labor-power in order to live, and enables the capitalist to purchase labor-power in order that he may enrich himself. It is no longer a mere accident, that capitalist and laborer confront each other in the market as buyer and seller. It is the process itself that incessantly hurls back the laborer on to the market as a vender of his labor-power, and that incessantly

converts his own product into a means by which another man can purchase him. In reality, the laborer belongs to capital before he has sold himself to capital. His economic bondage is both brought about and concealed by the periodic sale of himself, by his change of masters, and by the oscillations in the market-price of labor-power. (pp. 577–578)

Marx consistently points to the ways in which this economic bondage of labor—perpetuated through the labor-capital relationship—is mystified or distorted by bourgeois ideology in the minds of capitalists and workers alike. In his discussion concerning the accumulation of capital, Marx points out that in explaining the "original capital…advanced" to begin the process of capitalist production, the "spokesmen of Political Economy" (p. 581) are quick to point out that its source lies in the accumulated fruits of the capitalist's own labor and that of his forefathers handed down through inheritance. Somewhat sarcastically, we believe, Marx refers to this initial investment of any given capitalist as "primitive labor" (p. 583), which he himself qualifies with quotation marks. Because of the ongoing existence of primitive accumulation—which often takes the violent form of conquest and plunder and is conducted in the contemporary context under the guise of the war on terrorism and protecting democracy—Marx's use of the term "primitive labor" seems to be employed to challenge the myth of the hard-working capitalist pulling himself up by his bootstraps via the strength of his indomitable will and unyielding cleverness. Marx leaves the investigation of primitive accumulation for a later chapter. At this point in the text, he assumes the initial investment was made honestly. The story is quite different with respect to the surplus-value created during the production process: "with regard to the additional capital…how that originated we know perfectly well. There is not a single atom of its value that does not owe its existence to unpaid labor" (p. 582). As mentioned above, the very structure and process of capitalist accumulation itself and the almost passive role of personified capital increasingly leads to the subjugation and economic bondage of labor. This movement toward domination—and ultimately immiseration—tends to be accompanied by heightened levels of working-class awareness. This can cause an explosive brew of worker unrest just as capital is creating the conditions of its own demise or negation. The situation is thus quite contradictory, and it is for this reason that the ideological mystifications of the bourgeoisie are so important. In the end, what mystifies the exploitation inherent within the exchange between labor and capital is the ideology of the outdated equivalency laws of commodity exchange described above.

What Marx is uncovering here is the compounding nature of capitalism in which the money-form of the capital of today disguises the fact that its substance actually consists of the previous setting in motion of labor-power. Of course, this is a fact that tends to be hidden to both the capitalist and the laborer. However, because the material and discursive reproduction of the capitalist resides within capital's ability to expand, it is no wonder that "capitalist production not only creates a world of delights; it lays open, in speculation and the credit system, a thousand sources of sudden enrichment" (pp. 593–594). Situating this analysis within the historical development of capitalism itself, Marx, again, points to a system pregnant with negative potential, as it is propelled by laws of capitalist production operating behind the backs of laborers and capitalists alike:

> When a certain stage of development has been reached, a conventional degree of prodigality, which is also an exhibition of wealth, and consequently, a source of credit, becomes a business necessity of the "unfortunate" capitalist. Luxury enters into capital's expenses of representation. Moreover, the capitalist gets rich, not like the miser, in proportion to his personal labor and restricted consumption, but at the same rate as he squeezes out the labor-power of others, and enforces on the laborer abstinence from all life's enjoyments. (ibid.)

It is precisely this one-sided obsession with profit that will always lead the capitalist to reduce the price of labor-power whenever possible, even below its market value. Political economy not only prods the early capitalist to abstain from consumption when the rate of profit was in its low, nascent stage, it forever complains that the laborer's standard of living is too luxurious, too wasteful, and should be lowered. The capitalist will complain of the price of labor in one country as compared to another. Today's age of austerity has revealed the depth to which capital has gone in appropriating labor's necessary consumption fund in a capitalist economy facing the physical limits of a finite planet hindering its own need for infinite expansion. The creativity of the capitalist here is made possible by the elasticity of labor-power, whose price fluctuates above and below a middle-average point. The necessary opulent consumption patterns of the simultaneously real and symbolic 1% situated next to the growing global immiseration of the vast majority increasingly reveals something inherently destructive and degrading about the process of creating and perpetually expanding capital. This logic represents the very substance of capital's DNA, and it cannot be reformed out of capital. This is a contradiction of capital: as capital expands both absolutely and relatively, greater wealth also becomes increasing concentrated in fewer and fewer hands. This not only creates the objective conditions for rebellion and revolutionary movements, it also establishes the foundations of a socialist society.

The first step in revolutionizing capitalist production relations, as argued above, is to abolish capital's ability to accumulate surplus labor-time. However, to better understand the economic bondage of labor and how to overcome it, a closer examination of personified capital, the class that profits from labor's subjugation, is required. Consider:

> Except as personified capital, the capitalist has no historical value, and no right to that historical existence... And so far only is the necessity for his own transitory existence implied in the transitory necessity for the capitalist mode of production. But, so far as he is personified capital, it is not values in use and the enjoyment of them, but exchange-value and its augmentation, that spur him into action. Fanatically bent on making value expand itself, he ruthlessly forces the human race to produce for production's sake; he thus forces the development of the productive powers of society, and creates those material conditions, which alone can form the real basis of a higher form of society, a society in which the full and free development of every individual forms the ruling principle. Only as personified capital is the capitalist respectable. As such, he shares with the miser the passion for wealth as wealth. But that which in the miser is a mere idiosyncrasy, is, in the capitalist, the effect of the social mechanism, of which he is but one of the wheels. Moreover, the development of capitalistic production makes it constantly necessary to keep increasing the amount of the capital laid out in a given industrial undertaking, and competition makes the immanent laws of capitalist production to be felt by each individual capitalist, as external coercive laws. It compels him to keep constantly extending his capital, in order to preserve it, but extend it he cannot, except by means of progressive accumulation. (p. 592)

Marx's insights here are crucial. As the laborer ceases to exist as such with the abolition of surplus labor-time, so too does the capitalist cease to exist, for what makes a capitalist a capitalist is his appropriation of surplus labor-time. If capitalism has been necessary for elevating our productive capacity to the point where it can now easily support the existence of all of humanity, dramatically reducing the amount of labor hours each person needs to expend to reproduce her or his own existence, then the capitalist class has used up its historical necessity (as we do not endorse a teleological view of history, we are aware that noncapitalist methods could have achieved this, yet the fact remains that it is capitalism that we confront as both productive and destructive force). What is more, the values and motivations that animate the capitalist have no place in a society striving toward capital's opposite—that is, a society based on *use-value* rather than *exchange-value*; such is a definition of socialism. And, when this situation is negated yet again, use-value is liberated from this particular dialectic and instead becomes use. This, for us, is one possible definition of communism: the right to use. A Marxist pedagogy of becoming resists capital's insistence that the capitalist has a right to exist; he does not. His existence, the existence of capital personified in a real human being, together in a class of capitalists, causes the economic bondage and growing suffering of labor. Now, the capitalists may or may not (depending on the severity of their crimes and the set of laws that we developed and deploy to judge them) have a right to be alive as human beings, but they categorically do not have a right to be capitalist human beings. In other words, labor does not belong to capital, and the capitalist does not have a human right to exploit and degrade humanity.

In other words, we might summarize the above quote noting that in this discussion concerning the role of the capitalist, he or she has no place or right to be in a world without exploitation or systematic dehumanization and intellectual degradation. Contributing to his Hegelian dialectics of becoming, Marx suggests that socialism, where all of labor's material needs are met, can only develop out of a well-developed form of capitalism, a somewhat controversial point given the Soviet Union's transition from feudalism to socialism. Given the all-encompassing nature of capitalism today as a truly global system, we need not engage the Soviet Union debate here but rather note that new developments can only emerge from any set of given conditions and not apart from them or independent of them as some utopian critical pedagogues suggest. In the following discussion, we expand on the themes highlighted above, reflecting on their implications for our Marxist critical pedagogy of becoming.

Making the Capitalist Impossible

If the laborer, according to political economy, is nothing more than a *machine for producing surplus-value*, the capitalist, as we will examine below, is nothing more than a machine for transforming surplus-value back into the production process to accumulate more value. The laws of capital act as an *external coercive force* upon the individual human capitalists. The savageness of actually existing capitalism cannot be reduced to personality defects of the capitalists, as it is rather the result of the competition between capitalists driven by the logic of capital, the augmentation and expansion of surplus-value. This final chapter reaffirms the position advanced throughout this book—that the deadliness of capital is inherent to it, and while it can sometimes be kept at bay, it cannot be regulated out of existence. Consequently, a Marxist critical pedagogy of becoming refers to the potential within capitalism as both a positive potential owing to the massive productive capacity of the machine factory but also as a negative potential stemming from working-class resistance to the perpetually extending tendency toward alienation within capitalist production relations. As discussed earlier, Marx notes early on in *Capital* that initially, it is just the product of a worker's labor she is alienated from. With the advent of manufacture proper, the division of labor is extended and the intellectual capacity of the laborer is reduced as its function is transferred to the workshop. As the machine factory replaces the workman's tools and physical strength, so too does it replace his thinking. As a result, the workman becomes an automaton and is thereby alienated from his own intellect. In this movement, his dependency on and subjugation to the capitalist is rendered more complete. The human's material and intellectual wellbeing simultaneously suffer and experience severe degradation. Marx pointed to the reunification of mental labor with manual labor as a way to revolutionize production relations (i.e., abolish surplus-labor time and prevent systematic intellectual degradation) as a primary concern of a Marxist pedagogical project.

In accordance with the dialectical conception of historical change, Marx explains the initial ideological pressures on the capitalist as resulting from capital's own development and transformation. Political economy, that is, in capitalism's early stages of development, called on the capitalist to abstain from consuming too much of his revenue so that it could be thrown back into production. Such abstention was necessary for the expansion of capital because, early on, profit margins of English capitalism were low. Indeed, Marx notes that just about every new capitalist begins at this early, fragile stage of development, and the situation is similar today, at least with first-time "entrepreneurs." Through the eras of capitalist development, more generally, Marx reflects upon the ideological shift among capitalists, noting, "while the capitalist of the classical type brands individual consumption as a sin against his function, and as 'abstinence' from accumulating, the modernized capitalist is capable of looking upon accumulation as 'abstinence' from pleasure" (p. 593). As capital has undoubtedly already outlived its historical purpose of growing the productivity of human labor, the development of his personification contradictorily embodies his own negation. As stated above, the capitalist has no right to be.

The economists that came before Marx would have been shocked at the exuberant levels of luxury consumption of the most powerful members of the capitalist class of his time. So too would Marx be stunned by the opulence of the 21st century multinational capitalist, a small handful of whom own nearly the entire planet, a scale that is truly difficult to comprehend. Marx would not just be shocked by today's existing levels of opulent consumption by the 1%, but he surely would have been dumbfounded in the face of the levels of stockpiled dead labor (i.e., money) that is neither put into circulation nor re-invested. Accompanying this, of course, are levels of poverty and misery equally difficult to grasp. Future generations (and here we are taking the future for granted) will surely look back to our time and wonder how workers allowed their conditions to be degraded so low. That is, economists may wonder how and why laborers allowed the price of labor to be pushed down so far below its value. While the practice of transforming, "within certain limits, the laborer's necessary consumption-fund into a fund for the accumulation of capital" (p. 599) was a well-established practice during Marx's time, its contemporary levels of depravity can only be compared to the deadly practices of slave labor in the Caribbean and in the American South before the invention of the cotton gin.

While the internal laws of capitalist accumulation act as an external coercive force on the capitalist, it would hardly seem that today's mega-wealthy capitalists would need to be coerced into doing what they themselves brag about doing and are praised for doing by bourgeois society in general. It is the destruction of the romanticization of the world's plunderers and their assumed right to exist as such on which this Marxist pedagogy of becoming insists. In addition, we must not fail to also reject the romanticization of work and suffering as somehow inherently noble. In its place, this Marxist pedagogy of becoming pushes beyond the bourgeois clichés that tether working-class resistance to the reification of the labor-capital relationship, papering over the deadly mechanisms, desperately waiting to either consume and prematurely expend the physical laborer or imprison and/or exterminate him and her once and for all time.

Again, because the process of appropriating surplus-value is disguised by the money relation—that is, because it is concealed beneath the surface of wages, where it appears every hour of work is paid—not even capitalists are conscious of the existence of surplus-value. The capitalist, like capitalist-educated labor in general, only sees what the capitalist himself invests in capitalist production as one lump sum and sees no difference between constant capital and variable capital. One of the consequences of conflating constant and variable capital is that the bourgeois economist's calculation of the rate of profit is highly skewed, concealing the more extreme rate of exploitation. In chapter 25 of the first volume of *Capital*, Marx more explicitly investigates this notion of the rate of profit in the context of the rate of growth, outlining "the general law of capitalist accumulation" (p. 612). In this process, he offers a more complete view of capital as a process of accumulation, understandings central to the development of a Marxist pedagogy of becoming.

> Growth of capital involves growth of its variable constituent or of the part invested in labor-power. A part of the surplus-value turned into additional capital must always be re-transformed into variable capital, or additional labor-fund. If we suppose that, all other circumstances remaining the same, the composition of capital also remains constant (i.e., that a definite mass of means of production constantly needs the same mass of labor-power to set it in motion), then the demand for labor and the subsistence-fund of the laborers clearly increase in the same proportion as the capital, and the more rapidly, the more rapidly capital increases. Since the capital produces yearly a surplus-value, of which one part is yearly added to the original capital; since this increment itself grows yearly along with the augmentation of the capital already functioning; since lastly, under special stimulus to enrichment, such as the opening of new markets, or of new spheres for the outlay of capital in consequence of newly developed social wants, etc., the scale of accumulation may suddenly be extended. (p. 613)

The result of such sudden surges in production where the supply of labor used is significantly greater than the year before at times may lead to a situation where capital's demand for labor exceeds the supply, resulting in an increase in wages. The capitalist, of course, is driven by the desire to avoid this falling rate of profit at all costs. The wise political economist understands the crucial importance of a reserve pool of laborers that can cushion the periodic fluctuations in capital's labor requirements in order to safeguard against falling rates of profit owing to increased variable capital payments. Nations engage in empire building and go to war over access to this precious resource, this human commodity, as well as access to land, to what nature provides gratuitously, the raw materials out of which products, combined with human labor, are fashioned. Perhaps even more significant, because it operates perpetually and thus normatively with capital, is the enslavement of labor due not necessarily to colonial and military conquest but to the very process of capitalist production:

The reproduction of a mass of labor power, which must incessantly re-incorporate itself with capital for that capital's self-expansion; which cannot get free from capital, and whose enslavement to capital is only concealed by the variety of individual capitalists to whom it sells itself, this reproduction of labor-power forms, in fact, an essential of the reproduction of capital itself. Accumulation of capital is, therefore, increase of the proletariat. (pp. 613–614)

The laborer's economic bondage is tied to her freedom from the means of production and the dependency on the wage to survive. A Marxist pedagogy of becoming points to not only specific capitalists accumulating the most capital and committing the most severe crimes against humanity; it instead points to capital as a process as the real cause and greedy capitalists and immiserated laborers as mere consequences.

Conclusion

The only appropriate conclusion is the search for a way beyond the economic bondage and cynical recklessness of capital. Marx points to a higher stage of development where, initially, surplus labor-time is done away with. Eventually, time as a standard measure is also abolished and replaced with the living embodiment of *each according to her ability and each according to her need*. As this unfolds the laborer grows and develops personally, and eventually a culture of true freedom and independence emerges as mental and manual labor flourish together. Movement toward this vision is the process of transforming capitalist production relations into socialism and then communism, and the journey begins with existing capitalist conditions and relations. Freire understood that the capitalist, due to his position of privilege, will not lead a revolution against the process of amassing wealth of which he is the primary beneficiary. Contributing to this conclusion Marx comments on the inability of capital to even imagine a world without capital or a worker aside from his existence as labor: "the practical agents of capitalistic production and their pettifogging ideologists are as unable to think of the means of production as separate from the antagonistic social mask they wear today, as a slave-owner to think of the worker himself as distinct from his character as a slave" (p. 608). It is therefore those the capitalist stands before as an enemy, as an antagonist, those who rely on a wage to survive, who will continue the long struggle against dehumanization and for the revolutionization of capitalist production relations. Our Marxist pedagogy of becoming rolls back the bourgeois skin of ideological deception, challenging student workers to see and reflect upon capital for what it is—dead labor set in motion against living labor.

Again, along with this transformation, the capitalists' assumed right to exist as such is challenged. The former capitalist must not be permitted to continue living off of either accumulated reserves of or newly accumulated dead labor; all of this is expropriated. The former capitalist must expend his own labor to reproduce the value of his own existence and be encouraged to develop it along with his mental labor. In this way, the dehumanized and oppressing capitalist, for the first time, can become more human, as his mythical right to oppress has been repressed. While we have a consistent historical record demonstrating that the capitalist and owning class chooses to resist revolutions by any means necessary, we leave open the possibility that it could be otherwise. For it is through this process of becoming that the revolutionary working class, by abolishing the capitalists' right to exist as such, actually creates the conditions for not only their own liberation but the liberation of the capitalist as well. In the social universe of capital, the concept of what it means *to be* is defined as to be rich, which alienates the human from their own human potentials and dispositions. A more humanized conception of the process of *becoming*, focuses on the human, collectively engaged in community, each contributing to the reproduction of life based upon the ways her own specific abilities and interests can contribute to some degree of a shared vision of human existence. This ideal begins within the capitalist present and forever strives toward justice, even after the abolition of surplus labor-time and the communist future.

EPILOGUE: NEGATE THE PRESENT!

Every revolution seems impossible until it happens; then, it becomes inevitable.
—ALBIE SACHS
Everything under the heavens is in utter chaos; the situation is excellent.
—MAO TSE-TUNG

There can be no doubt that the contradictions of capital are everywhere heightening and intensifying. The extreme social, economic, and political inequality that characterizes the global situation can't be sustained for much longer. The objective basis for a revolutionary situation has been laid by capital itself. We cannot, however, predict the demise of capitalism, nor insist on the imminency of its collapse. Economic crises, ultimately, are not necessarily bad for capitalism. As Smith (1984/2008) observes, "crises can also be acutely functional for capital. The mergers, takeovers, and bankruptcies as well as the general devaluation (of commodities, labor power, machinery, money) and destruction of capital (variable as well as constant) that accompany crises also prepare the ground for a new phase of capitalist development" (p. 170). While—or rather, as—capital accumulation is necessarily expansive, it thrives on destruction. Capital has been able to produce, alter, destroy, and transform our world in so many ways over the course of its rule. We mention this not to foster despair but because we do not want to fall victim to the illusion of economic determinism, to the fantasy that the contradictions of capitalism will, on their accord and in their own time, usher in a new mode of production.

The economic crisis of capitalism only provides the objective basis for a revolutionary situation; the subjective factors must be cultivated. In other words, we need to turn the economic crisis into a social crisis and, ultimately, into a political crisis that is irresolvable within the current order. This is, we believe, precisely the task of revolutionary critical pedagogy. This pedagogy must take place on an epistemological and an ontological register. We need to demystify—that is, to reveal the class interests behind—the dominant ideology that is propagated through every facet of society, including and especially through the school system. Today, this demystification process necessitates placing education in its relationship to and within global capital and the global class war. Our understandings of the world, ourselves, and others inevitably come to shape our actions, our social relations, and our very being; in this way, epistemology and ontology are absolutely inseparable. While ideology critique is surely a necessary component of any revolutionary movement, it is not in itself sufficient. We think that critical education (including the educational left) has been rather unsuccessful—or perhaps unwilling—to move beyond critique. One of the upsides of the current attacks on public institutions of higher education, indeed, might be that they bring the barricades to the university, making critique for the sake of critique increasingly untenable.

Not only must critical pedagogy and educational theory stop tarrying at the level of epistemology, and not only should they be situated and engaged in social and political struggles; they also must imagine futures. Of course, one of the beautiful—if terrifying—attributes of becoming is that it cannot be predicted. We can't, at this moment, begin to imagine what could come of our passions, desires, and intellects once they have been liberated from the terror of capitalist production and its accompanying forms of life. Yet this should not prevent us from either investigating the process of becoming or articulating possible visions of the future. It is, after all, from within the present that the future can emerge; "everything," as Marx (1856/1972) said, "seems pregnant with its contrary" (p. 577).

Moreover, we can absolutely imagine and begin to articulate just ways to arrange the production, circulation, and distribution of value. We can turn to historical and contemporary examples of communities, states, federations, and unions that have overthrown the rule of private property; we can learn from their successes and failures. We can also envision what a new form of government would look like in the United States. The U.S.-based Party for

Socialism and Liberation (2010), for example, outlines some of the basic structures of what a "people's government" would look like. They put forward broad guiding principles and organizational structures of such a government, in addition to advancing specific laws, regulations, and policies to be enacted. To take just a few examples: "Elected officials of the new workers' government shall be paid an average worker's salary and shall receive no special privileges" (p. 13); "All occupations, military interventions and military proxy wars, agreements and alliances carried out by the previous imperialist government shall be ended immediately" (p. 15); "The new government shall honor all treaty obligations with Native nations, and shall provide restitution for land and resources stolen by the capitalist U.S. government" (p. 19); "Citizenship rights shall be granted to every person living in the United States" (p. 16); "The intellectual products of colleges and universities shall be the property of society, with no patents, trademarks, copyrights or private profit from social knowledge and materials" (p. 17).

We can and must imagine alternative futures from within the present; we can envision what expropriating the expropriators (the first act of negation) will look like and how it will take place. And while we cannot predict the moment of the revolutionary event or if it will be a failure or a success, we can orient ourselves toward it. In order to do this, we—critical pedagogues and the left in general—have to militate against the deceptions of economic determinism, of social democracy, and of reformism. These illusions, which take the inevitability of capital as a starting point, have resulted in an endless repetition of "criticism and interpretation, small projects and local actions, particular issues and legislative victories, art, technology, procedures, and process" (Dean, 2012, p. 174). Against this, we need to put communism back on the agenda as the indisputable horizon of the present, thereby reconfiguring pedagogy and politics, and insisting that we embrace the terrifying beauty of becoming.

REFERENCES

Allman, P., McLaren, P., & Rikowski, G. (2005). After the Box People: The Labor-Capital Relation as Class Constitution and Its Consequences for Marxist Educational Theory and Human Resistance. In P. McLaren, *Capitalists & Conquerors: A Critical Pedagogy Against Empire*. Lanham: Rowman & Littlefield.

Althusser, L. (1971/2008). Reply to John Lewis. In L. Althusser, *On Ideology*. London and New York: Verso.

Aptheker, H. (1974). *American Negro Slave Revolts*. New York: International Publishers.

Becker, B. (2008). What Do Socialists Defend in China Today? *Socialism and Liberation*, 5(1), 3–22.

Becker, B. (2013). Socialists and War: Two Opposing Trends. In B. Becker & M. Majidi, *Socialists and War: Two Opposing Trends*. San Francisco: PSL Publications.

Becker, R. (2012). *The Myth of Democracy and the Rule of the Banks*. San Francisco: PSL Publications.

Bell, D. (1995). *Brown v. Board of Education* and the Interest Convergence Dilemma. In K. Crenshaw, N. Gotanda, G. Peller, & K. Thomas (Eds.), *Critical Race Theory: The Key Writings That Formed the Movement*. New York: New Press.

Berman, M. (1982/1988). *All That Is Solid Melts into Air: The Experience of Modernity*. New York: Penguin Books.

Biesta, G. (1998). Say you want a revolution... Suggestions for the impossible future of critical pedagogy. *Educational Theory*, 48(4), 499–510.

Biesta, G.J.J. (2006). *Beyond Learning: Democratic Education for a Human Future*. Boulder, CO: Paradigm Publishers.

Biesta, G.J.J. (2010). *Good Education in an Age of Measurement: Ethics, Politics, Democracy.* Boulder, CO: Paradigm Publishers.

Blum, W. (2004). *Killing Hope: U.S. Military and C.I.A. Interventions Since World War II.* Monroe, ME: Common Courage Press.

Blunden, A. (2013). Contradiction, Consciousness, and Generativity: Hegel's Roots in Freire's Work. In Robert Lake & Tricia Kress (Eds.), *Paulo Freire's Intellectual Roots: Toward Historicity in Praxis.* New York: Bloomsbury.

Bowles, S., & Gintis, H. (1976). *Schooling in Capitalist America: Educational Reform and the Contradictions of Economic Life.* New York: Basic Books.

Burbules, N., & Berk, R. (1999). Critical thinking and critical pedagogy: Relations, differences, and limits. In T. Popkewitz & L. Fendler (Eds.), *Critical Theories in Education.* New York: Routledge.

Callinocos, A. (2011). *The Revolutionary Ideas of Karl Marx.* Chicago: Haymarket.

Canaan, J. Hill, D., & Maisuria A. (2013). Resistance in England. In Dave Hill (Ed.), *Immiseration Capitalism and Education: Austerity, Resistance and Revolt.* Brighton: Institute for Education Policy Studies.

Cleaver, H. (1991). Introduction. In Antonio Negri, *Marx Beyond Marx: Lessons on The Grundrisse.* Brooklyn, NY: Autonomedia/Pluto.

Cole, M. (2009). *Critical Race Theory and Education: A Marxist Response.* New York: Palgrave.

Darder, A. (2009). Teaching as an Act of Love: Reflections on Paulo Freire and His Contributions to Our Lives and Our Work. In Antonia Darder, Marta Baltodano, & Rodolfo Torres (Eds.), *The Critical Pedagogy Reader* (2nd edition). New York: Routledge.

Dean, J. (2012). *The Communist Horizon.* London and New York: Verso.

Du Bois, W.E.B. (1896/2007). *The Suppression of the African Slave Trade in America: 1638–1870.* New York: Oxford University Press.

Economist, The. (2009, Nov. 12). Nationalisation Rides Again. Retrieved from: http://www.economist.com/node/14859337.

Engels, F. (1880/2007). *Socialism: Utopian and Scientific.* New York: Pathfinder.

Feagin, J.R., & McKinney, K.D. (2002). *The Many Costs of Racism.* Lanham, MD: Rowman & Littlefield Publishers.

Foner, E. (1988). *Reconstruction: America's Unfinished Revolution, 1867–1877.* New York: Perennial Classics.

Ford, D. (2013). Toward a Theory of the Educational Encounter: Gert Biesta's Educational Theory and the Right to the City. *Critical Studies in Education, 54*(3), 299–310.

Ford, D.R. (2014). Spatializing Marxist Educational Theory: School, the Built Environment, Fixed Capital, and (Relational) Space. *Policy Futures in Education, 12*(6), 784–793.

Forte, M. (2012). *Slouching Towards Sirte: NATO's War on Libya and Africa.* Montreal: Baraka Books.

Freire, P. (1970/1998). *Pedagogy of the Oppressed.* London: Continuum.

Giroux, H. (1983). *Theory & Resistance in Education: A Pedagogy for the Opposition.* New York: Bergin & Garvey.

Giroux, H. (2013). Prologue: The Fruit of Freire's Roots. In Robert Lake & Tricia Kress (Eds.), *Paulo Freire's Intellectual Roots: Toward Historicity in Praxis.* New York: Bloomsbury.

Glazebrook, D. (2013). Libya and the Western Left. In B. Becker & M. Majidi, *Socialists and War: Two Opposing Trends*. San Francisco: PSL Publications.

Grande, S. (2004). *Red Pedagogy: Native American Social and Political Thought*. Lanham, MD: Rowman & Littlefield Publishers.

Gulson, K.N. (2007). "Neoliberal Spatial Technologies": On the Practices of Educational Policy Change. *Critical Studies in Education*, 48(2), 179–195.

Hardt, M., & Negri, A. (2009). *Commonwealth*. Cambridge, MA: The Belknap Press of Harvard University Press.

Harvey, D. (1982/2006). *Limits to Capital*. London and New York: Verso.

Harvey, D. (2005). *A Brief History of Neoliberalism*. New York: Oxford University Press.

Harvey, D. (2014). *Seventeen Contradictions and the End of Capitalism*. New York: Oxford University Press.

Haywood, H. (1958). *For a Revolutionary Position on the Negro Question*. Available at http://www.marxists.org/history/erol/1956–1960/haywood02.htm.

Haywood, H. (1978). *Black Bolshevik: Autobiography of an Afro-American Communist*. Chicago: Liberator Press.

Hegel, G.W.F. (1812/1993). *Science of Logic* (A.V. Miller, trans.). Atlantic Highlands: Humanities Press International.

Hill, D. (2013). *Immiseration Capitalism and Education: Austerity, Resistance and Revolt*. Brighton: Institute for Education Policy Studies.

Hudis, P. (2012). *Marx's Concept of the Alternative to Capitalism*. Boston: Brill.

Hudis, P., & Anderson, K. (2002). Introduction. In P. Hudis & K. Anderson (Eds.), *The Power of Negativity: Selected Writings on the Dialectic in Hegel and Marx*. Oxford: Lexington.

Inal, K., & Öztürk, H.T. (2013). Resistance in Turkey. In Dave Hill (Ed.), *Immiseration Capitalism and Education: Austerity, Resistance and Revolt*. Brighton: Institute for Education Policy Studies.

James, C.L.R. (1963). *The Black Jacobins: Toussaint L'Ouverture and the San Domingo Revolution*. New York: Vintage Books.

Jorgensen, G. (2014). Social Studies Curriculum Migration: Confronting Challenges in the 21st Century. In E. Wayne Ross (Ed.), *The Social Studies Curriculum: Purposes, Problems, and Possibilities*. Fourth Edition. Albany: SUNY Press.

Kahn, R. (2010). *Critical Pedagogy, Ecoliteracy, and Planetary Crisis: The Ecopedagogy Movement*. New York: Peter Lang.

Lazzarato, M. (1996). Immaterial Labor (P. Colilli & E. Emory, trans.), in P. Virno & M. Hardt (Eds.), *Radical Thought in Italy: A Potential Politics*. Minneapolis: University of Minnesota Press.

Lukàcs, G. (1924/2009). *Lenin: A Study on the Unity of His Thought*. London and New York: Verso.

Luxemburg, R. (2003). *The Accumulation of Capital* (A. Schwarzschild, trans.). London: Routledge.

Ma, B., et al. (2008). Precarious Is China's Socialism! The Chinese People Have Reached Another Extremely Critical Time! *Socialism and Liberation*, 5(1), 99–112.

Malott, C. (2014). Coming to Critical Pedagogy: A Marxist Autobiography in the History of Higher Education. *Journal of Critical Education Policy Studies*, 12(1), 117–142.

Malott, C. Hill, D., & Banfield, G. (2013). Immiseration Capitalism. In Dave Hill (Ed.), *Immiseration Capitalism and Education: Austerity, Resistance and Revolt*. Brighton: Institute for Education Policy Studies.

Tse-Tung, Mao, T.-T. (1966). *Quotations from Chairman Mao Tse-Tung*. Peking: Foreign Language Press.

Marcy, S. (1979). Global Class War and the Destiny of American Labor. In S. Marcy, *Global Class War*. New York: WW Publishers.

Marcy, S. (1990). *Perestroika: A Marxist Critique*. New York: WW Publishers.

Marx, K. (1844/1988). *Economic and Philosophic Manuscripts of 1844* (M. Milligan, trans.). Amherst, NY: Prometheus Books.

Marx, K. (1852/1972). *The Eighteenth Brumaire of Louis Bonaparte*. New York: International Publishers.

Marx, K. (1856/1972). Speech at the Anniversary of the *People's Paper*. In R. Tucker (Ed.), *The Marx-Engels Reader* (2nd ed.). New York and London: W.W. Norton & Co.

Marx, K. (1867/1983). *Capital: A Critique of Political Economy* (Vol. 1). New York: International Publishers.

Marx, K. (1867/1992). *Capital: A Critique of Political Economy: Volume 1: The Process of Capitalist Production*. New York: International Publishers.

Marx, K. (1875/2002). *Critique of the Gotha Programme*. New York: International Publishers.

Marx, K. (1885/1978). *Capital: A Critique of Political Economy* (Vol. 2). New York: International Publishers.

Marx, K. (1894/1981). *Capital: A Critique of Political Economy* (Vol. 3) (D. Fernbach, trans.). New York: Penguin.

Marx, K. (1939/1973). *Grundrisse: Foundations of the Critique of Political Economy (Rough Draft)* (M. Nicolaus, trans.). New York: Penguin.

Marx, K. (2007). *Dispatches for the New York Tribune: Selected Journalism of Karl Marx* (J. Ledbetter, Ed.). New York: Penguin Classics.

Marx, K., & Engels, F. (1845/1970). *The German Ideology*. New York: International Publishers.

Marx, K., & Engels, F. (1848/1972). Manifesto of the Communist Party. In R. Tucker (Ed.), *The Marx-Engels Reader* (2nd ed.). New York and London: W.W. Norton & Co.

Marx Aveling, E. (1896/2014). Introduction. In Friedrich Engels & Karl Marx, *Revolution and Counter-Revolution or Germany in 1848*. Eastford, CT: Martino Publishing.

McLaren, P. (1985). *Life in Schools: An Introduction to Critical Pedagogy in the Foundations of Education*. New York: Longman.

McLaren, P. (2005). *Capitalists and Conquerors: A Critical Pedagogy Against Empire*. Lanham, MD: Rowman & Littlefield.

McLaren, P. (2015). On Dialectics and Human Decency: Education on the Dock. *Open Review of Educational Research*, 2(1), pp. 1–25.

McLaren, P., & Farahmandpur, R. (2001). Teaching Against Globalization and the New Imperialism: Toward a Revolutionary Pedagogy. *Journal of Teacher Education*, 52(2), 136–150.

Means, A. (2013). Creativity and the Biopolitical Commons in Secondary and Higher Education. *Policy Futures in Education*, 11(1), 47–58.

Meltzer, M. (1967). *Bread and Roses: The Struggle of American Labor 1865–1915*. New York: Knopf.

Mészáros, I. (2011). *Social Structure and Forms of Consciousness: Volume II: The Dialectic of Structure and History*. New York: Monthly Review.

Negri, A. (1991). *Marx Beyond Marx: Lessons on The Grundrisse*. Brooklyn, NY: Autonomedia/ Pluto.

Negri, A. (2014). *Factory of Strategy: Thirty-Three Lessons on Lenin* (A. Bove, trans.). New York: Columbia University Press.

O'Flynn, M., Power, M., McCabe, C., & Silke, H. (2013). Resistance in Ireland. In Dave Hill (Ed.), *Immiseration Capitalism and Education: Austerity, Resistance and Revolt*. Brighton: Institute for Education Policy Studies.

Ollman, B. (1993). *Dialectical Investigations*. New York and London: Routledge.

Party for Socialism and Liberation. (2010). *Socialism and Liberation in the United States: What We Are Fighting For*. San Francisco: PSL Publications.

Payne, N. (2013). The Economics of Equality. In Edward Fort (Ed.), *Survival of the Historically Black Colleges and Universities: Making It Happen*. New York: Lexington Books.

Peck, J., & Tickell, A. (2002). Neoliberalising Space. *Antipode*, 34(3), 380–404.

Popular Front for the Liberation of Palestine. (2014, Aug. 19). PFLP Salutes the Black Struggle in the US: The Empire Will Fall From Within. Retrieved from: http://pflp.ps/ english/2014/08/19/pflp-salutes-the-black-struggle-in-the-us-the-empire-will-fall-from-within/.

Rikowski, G. (1997). Scorched Earth: Prelude to Rebuilding Marxist Educational Theory. *British Journal of Sociology of Education*, 18(4), 551–574.

Rikowski, G. (2004). Marx and the Education of the Future. *Policy Futures in Education*, 2(3–4), 565–577.

Rikowski, G. (2014). *Crisis in Education, Crises of Education*. A paper prepared for the Philosophy of Education Seminars at the University of London Institute of Education 2014–15 Programme, 22nd October 2014.

Ross, E.W. (2000). Redrawing the Lines: The Case Against Traditional Social Studies Instruction. In David Hursh & E. Wayne Ross (Eds.), *Democratic Social Education: Social Studies for Social Change*. New York: Falmer.

Ross, E.W., Mathison, S., & Vinson, K. (2014). Social Studies Curriculum and Teaching in the Era of Standardization. In E. Wayne Ross (Ed.), *The Social Studies Curriculum: Purposes, Problems, and Possibilities*. Fourth Edition. Albany: SUNY Press.

Rowlands, J., & Rawolle, S. (2013). Neoliberalism Is Not a Theory of Everything: A Bourdieuian Analysis of *Illusion* in Educational Research. *Critical Studies in Education*, 54(3), 260–272.

Small, R. (2005). *Marx and Education*. Aldershot: Ashgate.

Smith, D.G. (2009). Engaging Peter McLaren and the New Marxism in Education. *Interchange*, 40(1), pp. 93–117.

Smith, N. (1984/2008). *Uneven Development: Nature, Capital, and the Production of Space*. Athens and London: The University of Georgia Press.

Sperber, J. (2013). *Karl Marx: A Nineteenth Century Life*. New York: Liveright Publishing.

Thomas, P., & Reuten, G. (2013). Crisis and the Rate of Profit in Marx's Laboratory. In R. Bellofiore, G. Starosta, & P.D. Thomas (Eds.), *In Marx's Laboratory: Critical Interpretations of The Grundrisse*. Leiden and Boston: Brill.

Thompson, I. (2008). China's "Socialist Market Economy." *Socialism and Liberation*, 5(1), 87–98.

Vatikiotis, L., & Nikolakaki, M. (2013). Resistance in Greece. In Dave Hill (Ed.), *Immiseration Capitalism and Education: Austerity, Resistance and Revolt*. Brighton: Institute for Education Policy Studies.

Westheimer, J. (2014). Teaching Students to Think about Patriotism. In E. Wayne Ross (Ed.), *The Social Studies Curriculum: Purposes, Problems, and Possibilities* (4th ed.). Albany: SUNY Press.

Wilder, C.S. (2013). *Ebony & Ivy: Race, Slavery, and the Troubled History of America's Universities*. New York: Bloomsbury Press.

Young, P. (2013). Black Colleges and Universities: Their Past, Path, and Leadership. In Edward Fort (Ed.), *Survival of the Historically Black Colleges and Universities: Making It Happen*. New York: Lexington Books.

Zheng, B. (2005). China's "Peaceful Rise" to Great-Power Status. *Foreign Affairs*. Retrieved from: http://www.foreignaffairs.com/articles/61015/zheng-bijian/chinas-peaceful-rise-to-great-power-status.

INDEX

**Narrative, Dialogue
and the Political
Production
of Meaning**

Michael A. Peters
Peter McLaren
Series Editors

To submit a manuscript or proposal for editorial consideration, please contact:

Dr. Peter McLaren
UCLA Los Angeles
School of Education &
Information Studies
Moore Hall 3022C
Los Angeles, CA 90095

Dr. Michael Peters
University of Waikato
P.O. Box 3105
Faculty of Education
Hamilton 3240
New Zealand

WE ARE THE STORIES WE TELL. The book series Education and Struggle focuses on conflict as a discursive process where people struggle for legitimacy and the narrative process becomes a political struggle for meaning. But this series will also include the voices of authors and activists who are involved in conflicts over material necessities in their communities, schools, places of worship, and public squares as part of an ongoing search for dignity, self-determination, and autonomy. This series focuses on conflict and struggle within the realm of educational politics based around a series of interrelated themes: indigenous struggles; Western-Islamic conflicts; globalization and the clash of worldviews; neoliberalism as the war within; colonization and neocolonization; the coloniality of power and decolonial pedagogy; war and conflict; and the struggle for liberation. It publishes narrative accounts of specific struggles as well as theorizing "conflict narratives" and the political production of meaning in educational studies. During this time of global conflict and the crisis of capitalism, Education and Struggle promises to be on the cutting edge of social, cultural, educational, and political transformation.

Central to the series is the idea that language is a process of social, cultural, and class conflict. The aim is to focus on key semiotic, literary, and political concepts as a basis for a philosophy of language and culture where the underlying materialist philosophy of language and culture serves as the basis for the larger project that we might call dialogism (after Bakhtin's usage). As the late V.N. Volosinov suggests "Without signs there is no ideology," "Everything ideological possesses semiotic value," and "individual consciousness is a socio-ideological fact." It is a small step to claim, therefore, "consciousness itself can arise and become a viable fact only in the material embodiment of signs." This series is a vehicle for materialist semiotics in the narrative and dialogue of education and struggle.

To order other books in this series, please contact our Customer Service Department:

(800) 770-LANG (within the U.S.)
(212) 647-7706 (outside the U.S.)
(212) 647-7707 FAX

Or browse online by series:

www.peterlang.com